A Church of Islam

A Church of Islam

The Syrian Calling of Father Paolo Dall'Oglio

Shaun O'Neill

FOREWORD BY
Prof. Emma Loosley Leeming

WIPF & STOCK · Eugene, Oregon

A CHURCH OF ISLAM
The Syrian Calling of Father Paolo Dall'Oglio

Wipf & Stock
An Imprint of Wipf and Stock Publishers
199 W. 8th Ave., Suite 3
Eugene, OR 97401

www.wipfandstock.com

PAPERBACK ISBN: 978-1-5326-6727-5
HARDCOVER ISBN: 978-1-5326-6728-2
EBOOK ISBN: 978-1-5326-6729-9

Manufactured in the U.S.A.

For the people of Syria.

That they may have the strength to face the seemingly insurmountable challenges of today, and the vision and belief to forge a better future.

Listen to the story told by the reed,
of being separated.
"Since I was cut from the reedbed,
I have made this crying sound.
Anyone apart from someone he loves
understands what I say.
Anyone pulled from a source
longs to go back."

Rumi—The Reed Flute's Song

Contents

Foreword

As I SIT DOWN to write this, the world is reeling from another attack on Christians at worship. This time it was in Sri Lanka on Easter Day and, although nobody has yet taken responsibility, it seems likely that this was an act of sectarian, rather than ethnic, aggression; it has been pointed out that Sri Lankan Christians come from all ethnic groups in the country, and this has affected Sinhalese and Tamil alike. It is a reminder, if any were necessary, of the importance of meaningful dialogue and even more crucially, the need to learn to live peacefully and kindly amongst people of different beliefs and backgrounds.

This is the message at the heart of the Community of Al-Khalil, which was founded in 1991 by Fr. Paolo Dall'Oglio S.J. and Fr. Jacques Mourad at Deir Mar Musa al-Habashi, near Nebek, Syria. The Community was inspired by Paolo's dream of realizing Louis Massignon's blueprint for a Christian community whose vocation sprang from a deep love for, and understanding of, Islam.

The work of Al-Khalil is widely known in Francophone countries and in Italy, but is little discussed in the English-speaking world; the contrast is in many ways inexplicable, but that could be simply down to the fact that Catholicism is seen as more tainted by recent scandals in Anglophone societies. This has possibly made us less receptive to positive Catholic narratives like those of the Community of Al-Khalil. It is to be hoped that the current volume goes some way to redressing this situation by both bringing the life and work of Paolo and the rest of the Community to a wider audience and raising awareness of how Syria was before the current civil war. It should also give us hope that one day Christians will once again be able to live in peace with their Muslim neighbors, both faiths free from the persecution of extremists. Community members are the first to point out that their Muslim friends have suffered just as much as their Christian friends and relatives, and Jacques has gone further to argue that it is Sunni Syrians who have borne the brunt of *Daesh* atrocities over the course of the war.

Although in my professional life I study and teach the history and material culture of early Middle Eastern Christianity, my connection to Paolo and the Community is personal rather than professional. In my early twenties, I moved to Aleppo as a PhD student and took the advice of a fellow student to visit Deir Mar Musa. It was 1997 and at that point, Paolo and Jacques were the only fully-professed members of the Community, although there were a number of novices of both genders of both Syrian and European origins. As my studies progressed, I spent more and more time at Mar Musa, so that it seemed natural as my PhD finished to accept Paolo's invitation to live with them and organize an archaeological project at their new monastery of Mar Elian in nearby Al-Qaryatayn. I ended up staying for three years and only returned to the UK when Paolo gave me an ultimatum to take religious orders or leave. His justification was that the Community had grown so used to having me around that to stay any longer without commitment was unfair on an emotional level.

After leaving in 2003, I spent all my Easter and Summer vacations working at Mar Musa and Mar Elian until I began a new excavation in the east of the country in the summer of 2010. Little did I know when I left Syria that autumn that I would be saying goodbye to Mar Musa for many years due to war. Whilst I have been unable to visit the monastery, I have kept in touch with the Community over the last nine years and met regularly with members in Italy. Therefore, I have, to a small extent, shared with them some of the highs and lows of the intervening years.

I heard, like everybody else, the news of Paolo's disappearance in 2013 and hoped that it was a mistake. Then there was the déjà vu sensation when Jacques was snatched by *Daesh* in 2015, followed by the euphoria of his subsequent escape. Over the past six years, there have been many contradictory stories as to Paolo's fate but, as I write this, we still have no clarity as to what has happened to him.

I applaud the efforts Shaun has made in this book to try and present a rounded pen portrait of Paolo. To many he is a saintly figure who deserves consideration for future Church recognition. Others accuse him of taking a love of Islam too far and compromising on Christian doctrine to appease Muslim theologians. Some see him as a politically astute figure who made a valuable contribution to debates on the early course of the civil war, whilst others dismiss him as being naïve in believing that he could ever influence the Syrian government or the Islamists.

Both supporters and detractors agree that he is/was undeniably charismatic in the truest theological sense of the word, and that his motives have always been faithful and honorable. Having known Paolo and the Community almost half my life, my feelings are naturally more complex. I love him but can get annoyed with him in equal measure. I had many wonderful times at Mar Musa, but also had days feeling isolated and alone and did not always agree with Paolo's decisions.

The humanity of Paolo and Community members marked him and them as approachable and accessible. This is what made the difference for people when they needed help and support. What I mean to say is, Paolo is larger-than-life and stirs strong emotions in people, but to present him as a one-dimensional saintly figure is, in my opinion, reductive and takes away a lot of the color and significance of his life and work at Mar Musa. It is to be hoped that this work goes some way to giving a hint of just how charismatic, influential, infuriating, brilliant, annoying, and caring that Paolo can be.

Emma Loosley Leeming
Exeter
Easter Monday 2019

Acknowledgments

It TURNS OUT THAT writing a book, at least one that initially came screaming into existence as an MA thesis, is a little trickier than I had first thought. It demanded to be molded into something else, to coax the reader gently into its world of intrigue and religious diversity.

First and foremost, I want to relay my most humble thanks to those kind people who agreed to sit through innumerous hours of interviews with me: Fr. Jens Petzold, Prof. Emma Loosely, Prof. Ambrogio Bongiovanni, Shady Hamadi, Yasmin Fedda, Gianluca Solera, KM Alam, Prof. Edith Szanto, and Marius Kociejowski. Most importantly, I want to voice my heartfelt appreciation to Bashir, who observed, at length, life in the monastery of Mar Musa. This is the person to whom I owe most. I remain forever indebted to the commitment he shows, his unflinching belief in the good of people, and his courage and faith when confronted with adversity. He has taught me so much.

Without their patience, limitless energy, and enthusiasm, this book would never have come to fruition. I had always wondered how a stranger can convince participants to take part in such an undertaking; to trust and feel comfortable enough around someone to divulge personal and delicate information about a country that is still in the throes of war. Now I realize there is little persuasion necessary—they either believe in you, or they do not. They gave their precious time, relaying information on a variety of challenging, sensitive topics.

In addition to thanking my sources for their conviction and support, I'd like to shout out to Benjamin Peltier—Syrian

Coordinator for Amnesty International Belgium—for getting the ball rolling on this project back in 2017 and giving me the belief that I could complete it. Contacts of contacts from Benjamin paid enormous dividends. I owe him more than one strong beer, preferably onsite in one of those fine Trappist monasteries.

Others have made sacrifices that have collectively made a tremendous difference to my world. Håkan Bengtsson, for his wise mentoring, supervision and belief in me during my MA thesis—you are a gentleman and a scholar. My fellow theology students at Uppsala, especially Tanja Nannarelli, whose help with the English translation of Fr. Paolo's *Innamorato dell'Islam, Credente in Gesù* [Lover of Islam. Believer in Jesus], was as timely as it was succinct. Brian Palmer, who inspired me with his passionate words and vision for a better world, and the rest of the staff at the Theology Department, Religion in Peace and Conflict, Uppsala University, Sweden. My partner through the years, Karolina, who expertly walks that fine line between skepticism and support, and to whom I always listen, sometimes begrudgingly, for she is rarely wrong.

Paul McGinn, for his wise advice in putting me on the right path toward contacting the right people, and most importantly, for his second-to-none editorial skills (and doing it all with a big New Orlean's smile whilst on holiday). Declan Aylward, Laurence Dwyer, and Phil Soanes—friends anyone can feel lucky to have in their life—for precious feedback on various drafts I flung at them.

In a time of personal upheaval for me, there are several people who deserve a mention: Jerzy and Lidia Sanak, who opened up their home and offered it to me in true Deir Mar Musa fashion—a place of respite, serenity—so I could concentrate on the manuscript deadline. Bozena and Frank Maher—for selflessly giving me what was theirs, unconditionally, and, when needed, offering me the escape of sunny exotic climes. Frank's eagle eye and encouragement at difficult stages in this long process, showed me a chink of light when I thought all was darkness. My aunt Margo, for her support and psychological assistance. The towering John Kearns, for his awe-inspiring intellectual rigor, editing skills, criticism, and the occasional word of reluctant praise. Special word to Emma Loosley, for somehow finding the time between mammy duties and academic life to take a quick look through the manuscript, offering feedback, and compiling a foreword with little to no notice—you are a true hero. Adelina Krupski for helping with photo selection and map creation. Greg, Bogdan and Anton—brothers from other mothers—for their loyal friendship and help with promotion, translation, musical therapy, etc.

To all the staff and families in Deir Maryam al-Adhra in Sulaymaniyah, for their kindness, food, conversation, and unlimited tea. They took a disheveled Irish pilgrim into their community in Iraqi Kurdistan for three weeks—a touching experience in true Al-Khalil hospitality and genuine interreligious friendship. I will always carry this time with me. Barbora Tallova and Sebastian Dohnany—for their beautiful pictures of Deir Maryam with the largest telephoto lens I've ever seen. Jean Pierre Cecchini—for his humor despite the language barrier, and gorgeous pictures—merci mon amis! Fr. Jens, to whom I owe so much. I will miss our late night drives and chats across the rain-soaked Kurdish mountains. I hope to see you again one day my friend. To all the Community of Al-Khalil—thank you for reaffirming my faith in religion.

Lastly, to all my friends and family who have had to listen to me going on about this book over the last two years. Your suggestions, advice, and sporadic cold ridicule have all been equally helpful—respite at last! Your hearts are almost as large as your reserves of patience. Finally, I would like to thank my father and mother— John and Margaret—for being there from the very beginning, never judging, and always listening. This book is also for them.

Shaun O'Neill
Krakow, Poland,
April 2019.

Abbreviations

FSA   Free Syrian Army

IFD   Interfaith Dialogue

ISIS   Islamic State of Iraq and Syria

Prologue

THE DESERT SUN WAS still low in the east when a hooded figure clambered over the sharp shards of rock that straddled the Anti-Lebanon mountains of this part of southern Syria. He fell still. Vapory breath billowed out into the cool early morning air, his bear-like frame cast an elongated shadow that stretched out onto the beige stone beneath his feet. His right leg had almost finished bleeding after an avoidable tumble earlier in the half-light of dawn. How he had cursed and bellowed at his misfortune, but now his grumbling gave way to curiosity, for his eyes were fixed straight ahead. In the distance, the bosom of the mountain opened up before him and he could make out the faint outline of a structure at the edge of the escarpment below. It was 1982 and the young Jesuit had just come upon the ruins of a long-abandoned Catholic monastery called Mar Musa al-Habashi—Saint Moses the Abyssinian.

Emboldened by a love of Islam, the spoken word, and the heady pull of a long-coveted cigarette, Fr. Paolo Dall'Oglio's discovery reaffirmed a calling and vision he had long nurtured. Over the next three decades, the idiosyncratic Italian would transform this site into a religious and cultural center that would welcome all people as friends. In his monastic outpost, he would say mass in Arabic, champion interreligious tolerance, and extol the simple monastic tenets of prayer, manual work, and hospitality. The progressive message at the heart of the Community—charity, friendship and openness—would define his Interfaith Dialogue (IFD) work in the heart of Assad's Syria and beyond. These values would become the bedrock of the wider mixed ecumenical and monastic community of Al-Khalil which Fr. Paolo and Fr Jacques set about establishing throughout the region over the coming years. Unfortunately, the Italian's perceived radicalism in church circles would test his relationship with the religious hierarchy.

Since 1991, the Al-Khalil Community embodies Fr. Paolo's spirit and currently comprises several sister monasteries scattered around Syria, Iraqi Kurdistan, and Italy: Deir Mar Musa al-Habashi in Nebek (Syria), Deir Mar Elian in Al-Qaryatayn (Syria), Deir Maryam al-Adhra in Sulaymaniyah (Iraqi Kurdistan). It also includes the monastery of San Salvatore in Cori (Italy). (see map on page 50)

The monastery of Deir Mar Musa near Nebek, eighty kilometers from Damascus, would provide the grand setting for both formal and informal interreligious initiatives. It became a magnet for locals from the surrounding area—young and old, men and women, lay and religious, Christian and Muslim, Sunni and Shia. As the specter of war loomed and then enveloped Syria in a miasma of violence, Mar Musa also became a place of refuge for those fleeing the terror. Its door remained open when others' were bolted firmly shut.

By chance, I was lucky enough to meet Fr. Paolo in his beloved Mar Musa in February, 2011—just weeks before that calamitous war started. Many people have asked why I went to Syria at *that* time and I still cannot provide a plausible answer. It was not premeditated, rather it was a decision made in an instant. My love for the Middle East was always there, smoldering inside my chest since my very first journey more than 20 years ago. Most destinations held little of the intrigue and exoticism of a trip there: the sights, the sounds, the swirling sensory deluge that held me so captivated. I could never shake off my first glimpse of that early morning and late afternoon light—from Esfahan to Muscat, Amman to Jerusalem; the broad warm smiles and effusive hospitality, the delicious cuisine—rich and earthy, salty, yet subtle—the history, culture, architecture. The people.

Syria was the perfect encapsulation of all those qualities. It was the small selfless acts of kindness from strangers that moved me so; the young boy who without hesitation offered me his wooly ear warmers in Aleppo as the wind whipped down from the cita-del; the Bedouin family who ushered us into the warm confines of their stove-heated tent on a bitterly cold day in majestic Palmyra, feeding us sweet tea and dates as the snow fell outside; the spice seller who pushed free samples of his cardamom into my pockets under the shadow of Hama's famed Noria water wheels. I would savor that sublime aroma for months afterwards—the smell in-stantly transporting me back to the banks of the Orontes. I fell madly in love with the place.

Retrospectively, I cannot help but feel that something drew me to Syria at *that* specific time for some purpose. I booked flights, arranged visas, and jumped on a plane as the Arab Spring already rumbled, oblivious to the fact that Syria was lurching toward the edge of one of the most pivotal moments in its modern history. Events that would forever alter the country—and the wider region. My visit to Mar Musa on that sunny winter's day was made on a whim, a casual recommendation from a friend in Damascus. However, it stirred a tectonic movement in my life's trajectory that would usher me down a very different path. On my return to Eu-rope, I threw myself into following the story of Fr. Paolo and the Community. As each month passed, it took on more of a surreal, dream-like quality, and the deteriorating situation across large swathes of the country disturbed me greatly.

I then happened upon some notes I had scribbled down from my short stay in the monastery—at the time not realizing their future import. They would be the small seed that would later ger-minate as the inspiration for a Theology MA in Religion in Peace and Conflict that I completed in 2018. The thesis provided me an impassioned opportunity to catapult Fr. Paolo's vision and mes-sage of tolerance to a wider audience. I hoped that it might influ-ence and affect, inspire, engage, transform.

I would not have been able to produce this work without the help of many people who knew or worked with Fr. Paolo. I am indebted to others from a broad spectrum of religious denomina-tions who participated in or observed IFD activities in Mar Musa and the wider Community of Al-Khalil. Those who assisted my

research—whether witness, friend, or contemporary—often en-
dured hours of extensive interviews between January 2017 and
February 2019, providing me valuable insights into their experiences and recollections.

My sources included: Fr. Jens Petzold—understudy in Mar
Musa and now leader of the Community of Deir Maryam al-
Adhra, Sulaymaniyah, Iraq; Prof. Emma Loosley—Department of
Theology and Religion, Exeter University, who spent three years
among the Community of Al-Khalil in Syria and worked closely
with Fr. Paolo and his team there; Prof. Edith Szanto—Associ-
ate Professor in the Department of Social Sciences at the American
University of Iraq, Sulaymaniyah, who attended IFD seminars in
Mar Musa and remains a close friend of the monastery of Deir
Maryam; Prof. Ambrogio Bongiovanni—friend of Fr. Paolo and
Professor of Theology of Interreligious Dialogue in the Pontifical
Urbaniana University in Rome; Shady Hamadi—friend, assistant
and confidante; Gianluca Solera—writer, activist and close friend;
KM Alam—a Visiting Fellow at the Royal United Services Institute
(RUSI) specializing in the contemporary military history of the
Arab world and Pakistan; Marius Kociejowski—poet and author
who undertook several trips to Mar Musa and wrote about his
experience extensively. Lastly, Bashir,[1] who observed daily life and
Interfaith Dialogue in all its forms in Mar Musa.

I was humbled by the implicit trust they all had in me—a
stranger—from the very onset. To each of them I owe so much,
for without their priceless contributions, this book would simply
not have been possible. My commitment to ethics, honesty, confidentiality, and unconditional anonymity if requested—then, now,
and into the future—laid the necessary foundation for everyone I
interviewed. Needless to say, subject matter such as this is highly
sensitive in the context of the ongoing political crisis in Syria and
the various intelligence agencies involved. Guarantees provided to
participants had to be unequivocal as their willingness to contribute
to this project was often conditional; the trust they bestowed in me
was a responsibility that weighed heavily on my mind.

1. The real name of this source has been changed to protect confidentiality.

There was an urge to take a side step from the original academic work I had completed. By incorporating colorful creative non-fiction elements based on Fr. Paolo's intriguing interviews, journals, and talks, I have aimed to reinvigorate the original ethnographic-based thesis and harness the simple power of storytelling. This is a work firmly rooted in non-fiction—even the narrative elements that scatter the work are based on real-life events. While there may be an element of creative artistic license used to enliven the readers experience, the stories rarely stray from hard facts.

Just days after my brief visit to Mar Musa, in an unloved and smoky hotel foyer in the old town of Aleppo, I watched one of the first volleys of the Arab Spring reverberate out across the Muslim world on a small TV. Protests were enveloping Tahrir Square in Cairo. When I asked Syrians about the possibility of similar events enflaming their country, many laughed and brushed the suggestion aside casually: "Syria is different. Here the people are sleeping." How wrong they turned out to be. Within weeks the people would awaken from their slumber with a roar, pouring onto the streets in tides of discontent, engulfing whole neighborhoods with their demands for justice, and economic and political reform. They came from all sides of Syrian society, together chanting "al-Shaab Yureed Isqat al-Nizam"[2] (the people want the fall of the regime). The earlier unrest in Tunisia, Yemen, and Egypt would soon seem minor in comparison.

Upon returning to Europe, I watched in anguish at the images of carnage beamed into my home every night and the speed at which a country could morph. I felt impotent. It spoke to all our darkest fears—the indiscriminate and unspeakable turmoil of war. A generation of Syrians who would know only displacement and loss.

The spark had come in March 2011 when children from Deraa—a town close to Damascus—sprayed anti-government graffiti on walls near their school. They were arrested and tortured by the state security services—the *Mukhabarat*. This set off nation-wide protests for their release fueled by social media. The

---

2. Yassin-Kassab and Al-Shami, *Burning Country,* 36.

subsequent demonstrations were mercilessly met by live government fire. The funerals for the dead turned into surging, tense political rallies of immense scale.

When protests first broke out in Syria in 2011, as many as 30% of the Syrian population of 22 million were below the poverty line.[3] The effect of poverty was particularly acute in smaller towns and rural communities. Pre-war GDP per capita was already one of the lowest in the region at $3,300 per year, with over half of the labor force working in either agriculture or heavily subsidized state industry, and the country was feeling the strain of a refugee influx from both Lebanon and Iraq. At the time, oil, the big revenue earner, was ominously expected to run out within years. A couple of weeks after the initial protests, the boys who sprayed the graffiti were released, less one of their group who had been killed while in custody.

As protests continued to spread throughout the country, people sought justice for those murdered and detained. Additional political demands involved more civil liberties, less far-reaching powers for the security services, more political pluralism, an end to government cronyism and corruption, as well as lower food prices and more employment opportunities. Occasionally, protests also turned violent in response to strong government crackdowns on protesters.

In retrospect, Syria's leader, Bashar al-Assad, then had a window of opportunity to address the demands of the protesters at a critical moment in Syrian history. He could have allayed his people's fears by undertaking reform and tackling those underlying key issues at the heart of society. Instead, he paid lip service to people's genuine pleas, like lifting the almost five-decade-long state of emergency that had been in place in the country since 1963. Assad proposed vague, non-committal promises and blamed the popular unrest on a major conspiracy to overthrow his government directed from abroad. His claims would be ironically prescient given what would later actually unfold as the country was pulled into a civil war.

3. Cockburn, "Desperate Assad," line 58–60.

As well as a chronology of the interreligious efforts of the Community of Al-Khalil and Fr. Paolo's work and its origins, this book is also a eulogy to a Syria that no longer exists—at least not in the form that I witnessed during those fleeting moments of early 2011. The fate of many of those great people I met during that trip has driven me on to complete it—in their memory. I feel equally blessed and cursed, for that trip changed me, and my heart has been calloused by watching the suffering the people have had to endure. I knew a different country than the one which horrified nightly on the news broadcasts. Admittedly, any pre-war romantic idealization of Syria under Assad is redundant. It was a tough place to live—economically and politically—but it was still a safe and stable home for many, when neighboring countries were in flames.

As a direct result of the war, IFD initiatives have been sadly suspended in the monastery and visitor numbers have slowed to a trickle. Syria is in flux. The Community's programs remain a memory from the past of a country that sadly no longer exists in its previous incarnation. The fine, ornate tapestry of Syrian society—secular, sectarian, ethnic, tribal—has been engulfed in seismic upheaval. Nothing is as it was. Outside of the large urban centers, the country remains as I write this, still somewhat inaccessible, as the last scourges of ISIS[4] are banished from its eastern frontiers.

This book looks back through a present-day lens at a space in time where these interreligious events were happening and where it is now possible, retrospectively, to piece together the various actors who played a part in the organization and implementation of both the formal and informal activities. I considered the impact the monasteries' initiatives had on the local community amid the backdrop of the time—pre- and post-war Syria. I strove to decipher a holistic picture of Fr. Paolo—the genesis of the man and his calling, his interfaith work and political dissidence, his

4. For the purposes of this work, I will refer to ISIS and ISIL using the Arabic expression *Daesh*. Muslims use this term to refer to these extremist groups as they feel ISIS have coopted Islam through the use of the term "Islamic State." This linguistic difference separates the extremists from the vast majority of peace-loving Muslims' faith. *Daesh* is similar to the Arabic word *Daes* which means "to trample underfoot."

many flaws—against the social, religious, and political contexts of the time. I have drawn from multiple sources to supplement my interviews, including articles on his life, his book—*Innamorato dell'Islam, Credente in Gesù* [Lover of Islam. Believer in Jesus], in addition to colleagues' observations, analyses of private documents, journals, letters, audio-visual material, TV interviews, films, and online diaries etc.

Fr. Paolo published several books, journals, and pamphlets in Italian, French, and Arabic, of a theological nature. The paucity of writing by or about him in English has meant that he remains little-known in the Anglophone world. This obscurity is lamentable, and I sincerely hope that this book will go some ways toward bridging that gap. It has been occasioned by a desire to draw attention to his great human journey; from a highly respected and fiercely socially engaged Roman family, to his admiration of the pioneering work of de Foucauld and Massignon, to his immutable bond with Islam, infuriating obstinacy, spiritual fervor, and unshakable belief in the power of dialogue, tolerance, and non-violence. He was far from perfect, but that may have been part of his charm. By unearthing his interreligious vocation and love of the Muslim world, this book endeavors to celebrate not only the bright beacon of his moral leadership and compassion, but that of the wider religious Community. In doing so, I hope that it might illuminate this same path for those who dare to tread it in the future.

One of the most frustrating aspects has been to fully decipher, select, and utilize, with the ease and skill of a native speaker, the writings of Fr. Paolo on Deir Mar Musa, Syria, and Interfaith Dialogue. I have had to be extremely selective in my focus. However, as previously mentioned, one of the reasons I took on this project was that there was a dearth of information on Fr. Paolo and the Community in English, and I wanted to redress this imbalance.

My initial pool of participants provided priceless information, but was limited in scope. However, during the concluding part of my research and because of the implicit trust existing contacts had in me, more contacts came forward and I began to get greater access to the Community, which hugely enriched my work. Through these people, a deeper and more complete analysis of life on the ground in the Community was slowly revealed. I also had the opportunity of visiting another Al-Khalil monastery, Deir Maryam al-Adhra in Iraq, for several weeks in February 2019. My priority has always been to forge an objective and balanced piece that took on board as many facets of Fr. Paolo's life as possible, in order to illustrate where his influences naturally led him. Moreover, I wanted to showcase not just the work of Mar Musa, but the Community of Al-Khalil.

What is the legacy of Fr. Paolo's interfaith work and peace activism as the dust settles on a country ravaged by war? His direct castigation of the Catholic Church and Syrian state for their complicity in what was happening on the ground in Syria at the onset of unrest was noisy and defiant, when others were notably silent. Needless to say, his outspokenness had ramifications for the Community. After his exile from Syria in June 2012 over fears for his safety, he worked on diplomatic efforts for peace outside the country and remained fiercely political—to the chagrin of many.

The Italian's life, and the Community of Al-Khalil he helped establish, is a unique tale. Fr. Paolo, the figurehead and spokesperson for the Community, was very well regarded across all denominations in religiously diverse Syria, and was a beacon for interreligious tolerance and Christian-Islamic relations in a very troubled region of the world. It was a role he relished. Far from a fawning hagiography of Fr. Paolo, this work primarily remains a historical document that outlines the tireless initiatives of the Community of Al-Khalil. It is a salute of recognition to the nuns' and monks' bravery and steely determination in difficult, often treacherous, circumstances; it is also a rallying call for solidarity and love in these most troubling of times. Finally, there are the tragic events that unfolded after Fr. Paolo's clandestine return to Syria in 2013, and his subsequent disappearance from Al-Raqqah while reportedly negotiating the release of hostages. This is his story.

Chapter 1: Tilling the Soil

DUSTING OFF THE SMALL travel notebook that I had carried with me, I painstakingly try to decipher my hand-writing from that first visit to Mar Musa. Slowly, a more innocent Syria from yesteryear reveals itself.

First Impressions

Syria, February 2011.

They had kindly asked us if we wanted to stay. Even though we had met just hours earlier, it felt natural to accept. We look out over an endless moonlit desert plain that seems miles beneath us. We are the clouds which blow dark shapes across its pale surface. After the clamor of Damascus with a pre-dawn arrival that allowed us to catch a secret glimpse of that raucous, ancient, sprawl slowly waking up, the smell of freshly-baked *man'oushe* with a dusting of *za'atar* wafting through the crisp February air, the call of the muezzin from the towering minarets dizzying us with heady exoticism; here there is only the sound of the wind.

The monastery of Deir Mar Musa had been a recommendation from our pleasant, if overly chatty hostel owner who insisted it was a must-see. A sanctuary of dialogue between various faiths and cultures, a communal space of sharing and hospitality. We took a minibus to the town of Nebek and from there a share taxi dropped us to a dusty, exposed spot, beneath the rocky spires of the monastery where a few solitary goats eyeballed us curiously from the windswept verges of the road. The road was new. In the past a pilgrim needed to hike for several hours over the mountain from the neighboring village. The white sun blazed mercilessly—even in winter. It appeared as if steps had been chiseled into the mountain face, spiraling intimidatingly up hundreds of feet to the beginnings of some modest stone buildings that you could discern if you craned your neck skyward. To think of the place as a fort or a defensive structure of some kind seemed obvious. Later we found out that it had started life, many centuries earlier, as a Roman watchtower.

We were already becoming used to the imperious hospitality of Syrians during our first days wandering around the souqs and alleyways of central Damascus. "Welcome to Syria!" was the heartfelt refrain behind flashing iridescent smiles, so disarming that it was impossible not to be moved. One charming encounter after another, we smiled in turn, a little embarrassed but secretly proud of our new found fame. Syria's infamous label as one of the "axis of evil" countries did little for its reputation as a tourist destination but hardly curbed local people's enthusiasm. It was reason enough for us to ensure we left sixty minutes earlier for any appointment. They were fiercely inquisitive and we had lots of tea to drink together.

On entering the monastery that day, we were immediately greeted like returning pilgrims, and told where things were and what time lunch would be served etc. There was the reassuring hum of action. Both foreign and local young people were milling about industriously, doing various tasks in the garden, pruning trees, preparing food, cleaning, washing, organizing, chatting, singing. It was impressive. Amid the mania of activity, a sense of calm satisfaction imbued the place. We were introduced to the head monk, Fr. Paolo. His bulky frame was imposing, and this, in addition to his raspy Arabic, made him seem like a rather formidable figure. There was a no-nonsense air of efficiency about him. He spat out the language in haste, as if he couldn't stand for the damned words to stay in his mouth a moment longer than necessary. He rolled and twisted them as they ejected violently from his lips. The deep gravelly sounds of his hyper-enunciated rolling vowels echoed off the surrounding rock like gun shots. "An unexpectedly large crowd today. Now it seems we don't have enough meat for lunch! So be it. Blast. Lamb to the workers and rice for the visitors!" he barked unashamedly, before a generous meal was served up to everyone present, including those, like us, who had dropped by unannounced.

Fr. Paolo had rediscovered this place in the early eighties while studying in Damascus. The costly and lengthy refurbishment, undertaken over a seven-year-period, was his initiative and he had raised the funds himself. He was the seamless link between the Syrian government, local churches, and foreign NGOs,[1] in ensuring the vast renovation project had enough money, ran smoothly, and was completed on time. The Vatican and Italian and Syrian governments had also invested in the restoration of the beautiful thirteenth-century frescoes that adorned the simple church that nestled deep in the cradle of Mar Musa's amber mountains. We spent the rest of the afternoon exploring the labyrinthine corridors of the monastery with a child-like wonder. From the narrow western entrance where one must stoop upon entering, ancient stone chambers branched off, some leading to the small church and its rich frescoes with Arabic date inscriptions a thousand years old, others wound their way to a terrace perched precipitously on the cliff edge.

Later, as the inky blackness of a desert night sky fell on us without forewarning, we ate a small communal supper together—monks and nuns, workers, locals, tourists—and then shuffled in the darkness to our modest stone quarters. It was a silent world that was oddly reassuring. An enormous dome-shaped sky gradually appeared over our heads and the stars seemed close. Upon awakening in the blackness hours later, I desperately wished the toilets were as close as the stars had seemed earlier. Our little challenge involved lighting

---

1. The Syrian Department of Antiquities and the Istituto Centrale per il Restauro, Roma, were involved in initial restoration work. (Loosley, "The Community of Al-Khalil," paragraph 2.)

a candle in the dark, an accomplishment in itself, and then clambering up a makeshift ladder where a squat latrine had been hastily assembled. We had forgotten a torch. By now the moon had risen over the desert, banishing the stars' bright eloquence. The spectacle of that gloaming half-light illuminating the valley below was consolation enough for us.

The next morning, a group arrived early from the local village below—Nebek. They were mostly Muslim women, and some wore headscarves and giggled as they wandered around inquisitively. The impression was immediate and striking: a Catholic outpost deep in predominantly Muslim Syria, run by a team of charming monks and nuns who elevated simple hospitality as the guiding pillar of their work. We wanted to stay longer.

After breakfast, some of the monks were reciting the LORD's Prayer. After each line they left a pause which was then perfectly punctuated by a response from the Muslim ladies who happened to be praying at the same moment a little distance away. It was like a double incantation, an accidental antiphonal refrain. Seamlessly fusing two traditions, unconsciously. One culture. Two religions. A moment that was fleeting, ethereal. Both groups had become one organism, breathing in time, listening to their bodies' respiration, pausing and responding.

> *Our Father who art in heaven*
> *Allāhu Akbar*
> *Hallowed be thy name*
> *Allāhu Akbar*
> *Thy kingdom come*
> *Allāhu Akbar*
> *Thy will be done*
> *Allāhu Akbar*
> *On earth as it is in heaven*
> *Allāhu Akbar*

It was a hypnotic chant that carried us to another place with its warm and motherly touch. Momentarily, a beguiling togetherness embraced us all. The resonance of both prayers became joined in a holy union as the sound floated up the side of the mountain, its fleeting echo rising to the heavens—to God's embrace.

Paolo: Beginnings

Fr. Paolo Dall'Oglio was born in Rome in 1954 and both his father and mother came from well-known families in the area. His father was a lawyer and a high level functionary from *Democrazia Cristiana* who had worked on the land reform of Italy. He was also a *partigiano* in the resistance movement that fought against fascism in the Second World War, and came close to execution by the Nazis for his efforts. Paolo was one of eight siblings and the family was upper middle class, Catholic, intensely political, and well-connected. His home environment fostered direct social engagement and this activism was all spurred on by an urge to improve the common good of those less well-off. Fr. Paolo talked about his early life in an interview in 2003:

> "My father was very deeply involved with the Social Christian movement and I come from a background with a strong interest in social and political issues. I was a member of the leftside of the Italian Socialist Party as a young man. From an early age I was involved in movements like "Christians for Socialism" and the Boy Scouts."[2]

However, his studies to become a Jesuit did not always run to plan. While at the Massimiliano Massimo Jesuit Institute in Rome, his bullish nature put him at odds with the old order. It would not be the first time the headstrong Italian would have a brush with authority. After joining the Jesuits in 1975, he went to a war-torn Lebanon and Damascus to learn Arabic. He excelled and his linguistic prowess was renowned. He could not only speak fluent Arabic, but would perfectly take off an Aleppo or Damascene accent with such aplomb that people were convinced he was from

2. Loosley, "The Community of Al-Khalil," paragraph 9.

there. It appealed to his ego for he was a complete show-off and milked the compliments shamelessly. He studied theology and oriental studies in Naples and had a Master's degree in missiology from the Pontifical Gregorian University. His PhD from the same university was titled "About Hope in Islam."

While living in Damascus, a mentor had recommended the silence and peace of Mar Musa's site—a ninety-minute drive from the city—for a period of reflection. It was 1982 when he first encountered its ruins and it immediately enchanted, offering him the solitude and escape he had yearned for. The first period of renovation began in 1984, lasted until 1991, and was carried out only during the summer months. Afterwards construction was ongoing. The fresco restoration finished in 2003.

Fr. Paolo chose the Syriac Catholic Church as his rite when he was ordained a priest. It uses the West Syrian Rite liturgy and various rituals and practices in common with the Syrian Orthodox Church, is in communion with the Holy See, and has autonomy.

It is said that the name Mar Musa comes from Moses the Black (who probably founded the monastery in 6 AD), an Ethiopian prince and monk who lived in Palestine before arriving in Nebek and living as a hermit among the caves there.[3] According to Prof. Loosley, who lived among the Al-Khalil Community for several years, Fr. Paolo hotly disputed this. He claimed there were no images of Moses the Black before the eighteenth century and that the original dedication was to the prophet Moses. Historical evidence seems to support this theory.[4] The renowned wall frescoes and mosaics found in the chapel, date from 12 AD, and are regarded as some of the best-preserved Christian artworks in the Middle East. Officially, it remains the most complete fresco cycle still extant in the entire Levant.

The mixed monastic and ecumenical Community of Al-Khalil (friend of God) and the spirit that embodies it, founded by Fr. Paolo, Fr. Jacques, and their team in 1991, currently comprises

3. At this time estimates place 80 monasteries in Northern Syria alone. (Chaillot, *The Syrian Orthodox Church*, 117–119.)

4. Loosley, Interview.

several monasteries scattered around Syria, Iraq, and Italy. Al-Khalil was another name for the wider religious Community of Mar Musa near Nebek and its sister monasteries around the region—Mar Elian in Al-Qaryatayn (Syria) and Deir Maryam al-Adhra in Sulaymaniyah (Iraq). It also includes the monastery of San Salvatore in Cori (Italy). Al-Khalil means Abraham in Arabic—the spiritual father of the three monotheistic religions. Abraham is the biblical hero of hospitality and intercession (praying on behalf of others). Fr Paolo's ideas to push out the Community's interreligious message were grandiose and international. He was often seeking out potential sites for new centers, while persuading new postulants to seek admission to the Community as it sought to expand ambitiously.

The first seeds of IFD (Interfaith Dialogue) seminars in Mar Musa were sown around 1998 when the Community started their biodiversity seminars. Shepherds and farmers from the local area contributed to talks on animal husbandry, tree pruning, beekeeping, etc. Even then, the Community had an environmental focus and engaged with international organizations hoping to reverse the encroaching desertification in their vicinity and promote agro-biodiversity. The intended to co-align their environmental and cultural concerns with practical economic considerations by promoting eco-tourism. All schemes were undertaken in full co-operation with the local community.[5]

In 1999, they began organizing spiritual ceremonies. Later, during the winter of 2000, there was a historical seminar with a focus on ancient civilizations. There were various members of the religious community present. This all prepared the ground for the formal IFD sessions which started officially in 2003.

5. Loosley, "The Community of Al-Khalil," paragraph 3.

Early Monasticism and Christianity in Syria

There has been a long tradition since early times of solitary religious figures living in the caves of the area and building small communities. Even as early as 4 AD, Christian hermits were setting up monasteries where prayer, life, and work were organized by communities led by a spiritual father.[6] There is a rich history of monasticism within the Syrian Christian tradition over the centuries, with a focus on spirituality and asceticism. "Before the Schism of Chalcedon (451), eremitic and monastic life was organised in the hills and mountains around Antioch, Apamea, Cyrrhus, Tur Abdin, Persia. Monastic life was particularly vigorous in that area from the 6th to the 12th century."[7] Records show that Syriac culture at this time was rich and thriving, with many monks contributing to its development in literature, transcribing and translating texts, building well-stocked libraries and teaching in schools; they also cared for the sick and helped the poor and elderly. As a result, the monks who inhabited the area greatly added to the fabric of local, social, and intellectual life and were very highly regarded.

Today in Mar Musa, and other monasteries of the region, that rich legacy lives on. Syriac is a Christian dialect of Aramaic and it later became the liturgical language of Syrian Christians. Thus, the language of Syrian Aramaic or Syriac is intrinsically connected to Syrian Orthodox monasticism, with many old religious texts also being preserved in it. However, it is more common for Catholics to speak and say mass in Arabic, but Syrian Catholics also speak Syriac. This is one way to distinguish them from Greek Catholics who only use Arabic. Interestingly, even though Mar Musa was a Syrian Orthodox monastery until the mid-nineteenth-century (1868), many of the frescoes in the small chapel have Arabic inscriptions on them.

Author, Christine Chaillot, confirms that there is a plethora of names in Syriac for the various types of monks: "Ihidoyo (hermit/

6. Chaillot, *The Syrian Orthodox Church,* 112.

7. Chaillot, *The Syrian Orthodox Church,* 112.

ascetic), Estunoyo (stylite), Shmitoyo (barefoot), Rahoto (a wandering monk or missionary), Turoyo (mountain dweller), Madbroyo (desert dweller), Hbishoyo (recluse), Abilo (mourner)."[8] One famous monk, St. Simeon Stylites, who lived atop a column (a form of ascetical life quite common in Syria), re-energized monasticism, with both rich and poor seeking out his spiritual advice and healing powers.[9] Fr. Paolo mentions the latter regarding his first encounter in Mar Musa, "In August 1982 I undertook a ten day spiritual retreat at Deir Mar Musa and I felt that the intercession of St. Simeon Stylites had been effective when I received three apostolic directives."[10]

Syrian Christian monasteries during this period were centers of culture and education, often with schools of theology and fine libraries; they offered spiritual counsel, shelter, and charity when needed. The modern incarnation of Mar Musa and the Community of Al-Khalil was in many respects heir to previous ancient monastic settlements in its outlook and eccentricity. Its monks and nuns held some remarkably progressive attitudes on the religious *other*. A path can be sketched to find the modern genesis of these principles and those who paved the way for such a philosophy.

Tracing Footprints: From de Foucauld to Massignon

Two of the most prominent influences on the calling and vision of Fr. Paolo were Charles de Foucauld (1858–1916) and Louis Massignon (1883–1962).

Massignon was a famed Catholic academic of Islam who was a pioneer in cross-religious understanding between Muslims and Christians. No scholar was more influential in paving the way for modern Interfaith Dialogue efforts as Massignon, a man whose "religious practice was intimately intertwined not just

8. Chaillot, *The Syrian Orthodox Church*, 112.

9. Chaillot, *The Syrian Orthodox Church*, 112.

10. Loosley, "The Community of Al-Khalil," paragraph 12.

with Islam but with Muslims."[11] He dedicated his life to this ideal, with a strong academic focus on Islamic and Christian mystical thought, especially in the Sufi traditions.[12] Sufism is an integral component of Islam and both Sunni and Shia can be Sufi. It has a focus on inwardness, spiritual development, and a life of con-templation—values that would also be close to the Community of Al-Khalil and Fr Paolo.

In fact, Massignon spent fifty years of his life studying and documenting the life of the Sufi mystic, saint, and martyr of Islam, al-Hallaj.[13] Together with his colleague Mary Kahil, he founded the *Badaliya*—a pioneering interfaith prayer movement empha-sizing solidarity between Muslims and Christians at a difficult period in history, that saw colonial expansion consumed huge swathes of the Arab world in an insatiable quest for resources. The *Badaliya* movement was a precursor to the ideals of 1965's Vatican II decree, *Nostra Aetate,* as it advocated using the power of faith practically towards spreading peace and justice (Massignon was a vocal adherent of Gandhi), including striving for mutual respect and understanding.

Massignon, like Fr. Paolo after him, was inspired by the life and message of Charles de Foucauld, a French Catholic missionary who lived among the nomadic people of the Tuareg in the desert of Algeria. De Foucauld had dedicated his life to the Berber tribes of the region, and Massignon often sought out the French monk's spiritual guidance, once admitting that de Foucauld was very much an "older brother"[14] figure for him. Massignon and Fr. Paolo were moved by the simple life and ascetic philosophy of the French hermit and missionary. They would often quote him as a profound influence on their life's teaching and philosophy, citing his intense spiritualism, the modest and humble life he led, and his vocation to the desert of Algeria in the midst of Islam.

11. Buck, *Louis Massignon,* Kindle Loc.50.

12. Buck, *Louis Massignon,* Kindle Loc.53.

13. Buck, *Louis Massignon,* Kindle Loc.89.

14. Buck, *Louis Massignon,* Kindle Loc.190.

Like Fr. Paolo, de Foucauld was also a Catholic priest living in a predominantly Muslim country; both men shared common principles and their lives had several parallels. In a letter to a friend, de Foucauld once wrote, "I am preparing the ground, others will sow, others will reap."[15] He lived for three months of the year on a high, isolated peak in Algeria called Assekrem,[16] ten thousand feet above sea level, surrounded on all sides by the Muslim people of the nomadic Tuareg. A Christian outsider deep in the inner sanctum of Islam. He said of his fine mountaintop spot where he worshiped God, "It is so pleasant and so healthy to set oneself down in solitude, face to face with the eternal things; one feels oneself penetrated by the truth."[17] He had discovered a physical manifestation of the spiritual solitude he had sought out. A pursuit that had spanned much of his life had been sated. In several aspects, his journey and fate was analogous to Fr. Paolo's spiritual pilgrimage to Syria a century later.[18]

The parishioners of Nebek near Mar Musa, like de Foucauld's, were mostly Muslim. They would often visit Fr. Paolo's little Catholic enclave which promoted openness and hospitality, high up on the rock that nestled the monastery's humble stone buildings. Ali Merad, Muslim scholar, also writes of de Foucauld, "Nomad families from the surrounding valleys made the rocky ascent to the hermitage to visit the Christian marabout and to share his humble fare while they watched the sunset together."[19] The ascent to Mar Musa was indeed steep and rocky, though less challenging and inaccessible—making it even more popular with the locals. The Christian monastery has always played a special role in Islamic

---

15. Hamilton in Merad, *Christian Hermit*, Kindle Loc.150.

16. Merad, *Christian Hermit*, Kindle Loc.134.

17. Merad, *Christian Hermit*, Kindle Loc.134.

18. On December 1, 1916, Charles de Foucauld was tragically murdered by armed bandits who had intended to take him hostage. His life and death would inspire others to take up similar religious vocations. (Merad, *Christian Hermit*, Kindle Loc.141.)

19. Merad, *Christian Hermit*, Kindle Loc.136.

society and was regarded as symbolically sacred. It had a social function with Christians and Muslims often visiting together.

Early Days: Origins of a Spiritual Calling to Islam

There is a natural lineage clearly traceable down through the generations, a passing of this mantle from Massignon and de Foucauld to Fr. Paolo. They shared a vocational urge to be spiritual adherents of Jesus before Muslims, to be Christian witnesses for Islam.[20] Fr. Paolo's choice of the Syriac Catholic Rite for his ordination is telling, as, according to him, it was the closest to the rhythm and chanting of the Muslim sheikhs. The magnetism of Islam, and the pull of its mystical and spiritual element, was already evident even at this early stage in his religious life.

The origins of Fr. Paolo's calling to immerse himself in Islam emerged from several sources. The Jesuits focused on their sixteenth-century theologian founder, Ignatius of Loyola, and his Spiritual Exercises. This was a prescriptive, "how-to" text[21] of meditation, whereby one could empty the mind completely and induce a form of divine communication—directly with God. It was in this deep meditative state, lasting for hours at a time, that the young Fr. Paolo had a profound vision that would forever change the course of his life. He experienced a spiritual epiphany around 1975 or 1976 when he saw the word *Islam* emblazoned across his mind while doing the meditative exercises of the Spaniard Jesuit. A central tenet of these exercises is discernment—a type of mystical union with God and the believer. Discernment can also be deemed a way of channeling subjective ethical thought, a process of seeking out God in everything. Apparently, Fr. Paolo then talked to his spiritual director about this vision and he actively encouraged him to go towards his calling, to recognize the full extent of his vocation within a vocation. God, through these spiritual encounters, was inviting

20. Merad, *Christian Hermit,* Kindle Loc.585.
21. De Nicolas, *Ignatius De Loyola,* 100.

him to participate in dialogue with Islam.[22] It is important not to underestimate the weight that this spiritual encounter had on the young Jesuit's life and the path he would later follow.

This pivotal moment reaffirmed and bolstered the young priest's spiritual sensibility and set his life's compass towards the East and the people of Syria. It was here he would fulfill his calling. The young 23-year-old was steadfast: he wanted to offer up his life for the salvation of Muslims.[23]

De Foucauld once remarked, "I liked Islam very much, with its simplicity, simplicity of dogma, simplicity of hierarchy, simplicity of morality."[24] This aligned with Fr. Paolo's own love of Islam which sprang from its modesty, its chanting sermons, its underlying spiritualism, and one of its core tenets—hospitality.[25] He had this inherent closeness to Islam because of his spiritual vocation from God. Often people would tease him about converting. He would answer, "I am guided towards Islam because I have encountered the risen Jesus Christ. I cannot cut off my nose to spite my face."[26] For Fr. Paolo, like de Foucauld and Massignon before him, the spiritual attraction to Islam was natural and effortless. He felt culturally, linguistically, and symbolically[27] at home in this world. He was already thinking of a longer term goal. "I started to think how to transform the presence of the Church in the Islamic world into a Church *for* the Islamic world,"[28] he once exclaimed.

Charles de Foucauld and Fr. Paolo, both strangers in strange lands, had steadfastly renounced one life and embraced a very different one. They had both moved abroad and followed their callings. Muslims would appreciate the noble weight of such acts; that and the men's commitment, their belief in Abrahamic hospitality, their work ethic, their modesty, their spiritual devotion and

---

22. Bashir, Interview.

23. Dall'Oglio, *Innamorato dell'Islam*, 4.

24. Merad, *Christian Hermit*, Kindle Loc.612.

25. Bashir, Interview.

26. Bashir, Interview.

27. Dall'Oglio, "In Praise of Syncretism." paragraph 29.

28. Loosley, "The Community of Al-Khalil," paragraph 10.

passion for Jesus, all made strong impressions in the minds of their Muslim parishioners. To imitate the life of Jesus is for Muslims one of the most profound and authentic ways to espouse the message of the Gospel and it was something that resonated with people. Charity, humility, giving up the pleasures of this world and devoting yourself to the service of the poor and unfortunate are virtues that have always strongly impressed Muslims.[29]

Both de Foucauld and Fr Paolo believed in the Nazarean philosophy of austerity and simplicity. If de Foucauld was someone whose inner fire was love for Jesus and a passion to imitate his life,[30] then Fr. Paolo was undoubtedly his equal in terms of his raw unflinching belief in the necessity of following in Jesus' footsteps and tracing that same humble path. These two men, 100 years separating their lives, tried to seek out the common ground of spirituality that Christianity and Islam shared based on brotherly love. It was an ideal that aimed at transcending rigid and conservative religious boundaries and doctrine, to forge ahead with a space that was a modern-day encapsulation of interreligious friendship.

Men who made such sacrifices and left the creature comforts of a familiar, safe, predictable life, to travel far away to a foreign place, in often difficult conditions, to preach the simple message of Jesus, through actions not merely words, would always be noteworthy. On leaving his native Italy, Fr. Paolo said, "I left the country of my birth, where I have a father and a mother, which I grew up in and loved, following my longings, my obligations (. . .) and came to Syria. If the first country is the Mother Land, then this one is the Bride Land."[31] Syria and its people enchanted him. It was home.

---

29. Merad, *Christian Hermit*, Kindle Loc.305.

30. Merad, *Christian Hermit*, Kindle Loc.205.

31. Dall'Oglio, "Interview on Al Arabiya," 04:50.

Syria: Religious Mosaic/Political Monolith

There can be no discussion of early Interfaith Dialogue in Syria without some background on the historical, political, and religious roots of the country. Double-crossed and divided by the French and British in the Sykes-Picot agreement in 1916, many Syrians believed that after the Arab revolt (1916–1920), a single Arab state should have been created that encompassed not only Syria, but also Lebanon, Jordan, Israel, the West Bank and Gaza in one entity—*bilad ash-sham*.[32] Many felt betrayed by colonial powers that had placed their geo-political interests ahead of the people. Subsequently, Arab identity and domestic politics were the monolithic pillars that kept alive resentment at the mutilation of this concept. The unjust dissolution of the Arab world under imperialism was a lightning rod for those in authority.[33]

The Ba'ath party of Bashar al-Assad, and his father Hafez before him, have dominated Syrian politics for over half a century. The ruling elite of Assad's Syria—the Alawites—come from a minority branch of Shia Islam and represent 11.5 percent of the Syrian population.[34] Almost 70 percent of the population are Sunni Muslims, with Christians and Druze making up the remainder.[35] Assad's Ba'athist government managed for a time to balance this potentially explosive discrepancy by ensuring senior army and state positions were not purely Alawite-dominated. As a result, in the Syrian army and throughout the various arms of government and state-led institutions, Christians, Druze, and of course Sunni members abound. In fact, since the Ba'ath party took control in 1963, members of these disparate religious communities all played a prominent political role,[36] with a strong emphasis being placed on the secular nature of Ba'athist Arab nationalism. The party aspired to a socialist-leaning society that would judge all Arabs as

32. Hinnebusch, *Syria: Revolution from Above*, 18.

33. Hinnebusch, *Syria: Revolution from Above*, 159.

34. Van Dam, *The Struggle for Power in Syria*, 1.

35. Van Dam, *The Struggle for Power in Syria*, 1.

36. Van Dam, *The Struggle for Power in Syria*, 7.

equal, regardless of religious denomination. According to author Flynt Leverett, Bashar's father, Hafez, set great store in the "secularization of political and social life and its commitment to religious freedom."[37] It was one of the bedrocks of Ba'athism.

In this sense, the modern Syria that Assad inherited from his late father was, at least outwardly, a secular country; the big population centers had an influential and wealthy Sunni merchant class—the economic power house of the country—and the army was religiously pluralist. Writer, academic, and Middle East expert, Joshua Landis wrote in 2003, "Syria has been good to its minorities, who enjoy greater security and opportunity than in any other Arab country."[38] Dutch author and respected scholar on the Middle East, Nicolas Van Dam, insists that Ba'athist ideology was somewhat blinkered in that it denied existing social realities,[39] and brushed long-standing sectarian, ethnic, and tribal differences—both economic and social—under the carpet.

Landis talked in 2003 about the almost exclusively Sunni-focused and unbending Islamic education system of the country, which did little to build interfaith awareness and tolerance of the religiously *other*. In his view, such a system failed to facilitate the continuation of policies of religious inclusion.[40] He sounded a note of concern on the shortcomings of interreligious learning and dialogue at the school level across the country, and wondered how long "Syria's reputation for tolerance and willingness to protect religious minorities will survive its Alawite ascendancy."[41] Come the Spring of 2011, his note of warning would prove to be disquietingly prescient.

37. Leverett, *Inheriting Syria*, 25.
38. Landis, "Islamic Education in Syria," 2.
39. Van Dam, *The Struggle for Power in Syria*, 15.
40. Landis, "Islamic Education in Syria," 2.
41. Landis, "Islamic Education in Syria," 2.

Chapter 2: **Planting Seeds of Friendship**

Interfaith Dialogue (IFD): Background

TODAY, WHEN WE THINK of the Middle East, it conjures images of sectarian instability. However, it is easy to forget that for hundreds of years, people of different religious creeds—Christians, Muslims, and Jews, of various sects and denominations—lived in relative peace there. Peaceful interfaith coexistence has always been a part of the cultural and social tapestry of the different religious groups residing in the region. The very lifeblood of the Middle East are those things which everyone shares—experiences, practices, prayer, ritual, values, humanity.

IFD is undoubtedly a uniquely twentieth-century response to a twentieth-century challenge. There have been sporadic moments of dialogue over the years, but a movement exclusively aimed at mutual understanding between the creeds has only emerged in the second half of the twentieth century.

Sadly, some feel that IFD offers no way forward and provides no catalyst for change with those in positions of religious and political authority. Irrespective, countless advocates across disparate countries and religions have shown, and continue to show that IFD, though still in its developmental phase in many respects, can be a tool of immense power if harnessed correctly. It can build bridges when those around want to burn them—literally and figuratively. Religion still remains a rallying point for people in society as it has both integrity and credibility in many people's eyes—priceless values in today's modern world.

Dialogue is a grassroots set of egalitarian practices which aims to nurture long-term relationships based on mutual respect. The emphasis is on caring, communication, relationships, and understanding.[1] Dialogue is also a form of religious discipline. It seeks to get to know the *other*. Engagement with the *other* is its lifeblood, a place where we can foster real relationships with our neighbors that transcend religious divides.

It is also important to denote the difference between dialogue and debate. The driving purpose behind most dialogue should be some form of mutual understanding, while the term debate remains more individualistic in its approach, trying as it does to cajole or convince. True dialogue should never be superior in tone nor should it try to preach or convert; instead the emphasis should be on the celebration of religious difference and compassion.

As early as 1965, the Catholic Church recognized the intrinsic value of dialogue with other non-Christian religions with the groundbreaking Vatican II decree—*Nostra Aetate*.

Nostra Aetate: History

The Catholic foundation for contemporary IFD efforts was *Nostra Aetate*—the 1965 declaration on the relationship of the Catholic Church to non-Christian Religions. It was a much-celebrated decree from the Second Vatican Council which looked at the deepening relationship and shared bonds between religions around the world. It marked a pivotal moment in the development of the Catholic Church's more progressive stance on how it viewed other monotheistic religions, particularly, Islam and Judaism.

Islam is an Abrahamic religion and therefore shares a commonality in its cultural background and some of its beliefs—like ethical monotheism and the worship of a single creator. It shares common stories about Abraham from accounts in the Qur'an. Abraham is also the common patriarch for all Christians, Muslims, and Jews. YHWH, God, and Allah, are all at the core of these

---

1. Abu-Nimer et al., *Unity in Diversity*, 2.

religions, as are values of the divine, like mercy, justice, omniscience, and a negation of idolatry.[2] There are also shared religious figures, in addition to Abraham, that are common to all three faiths: Adam, Moses, David, Jesus, Joseph, Ishmael etc.[3] *Nostra Aetate*, along with the pioneering work of de Foucauld and Massignon, were indeed the sparks that lit the flame of the modern Interfaith Dialogue movement.

Nostra Aetate was a move towards a more pluralistic and inclusivist approach to faith, as well as a more liberal redefinition of traditionally rigid religious doctrine. It was the church openly stating that, actually, Muslims were not that different from Christians. Prof. Bongiovanni, theologian and friend of Fr. Paolo, notes that the political climate at the time was conducive to the decree (the Israel and Palestine issue). "This change needs to be put in the context of global change and the concern for the *other*—other religions," he states. "A change in the church's language when talking about the *other* is key in understanding the decree."[4] This kind of language can be seen even earlier. The publication of *Lumen Gentium: Dogmatic Constitution on the Church*, from November 1964, was a precursor to *Nostra Aetate*, It set an important precedent in the development of the more open attitude to Islam the church advocated, as well as the more moderate and inclusive language it put forward.

Nostra Aetate's decree proclaimed that all non-Christian monotheistic religions around the world shared one thing: they all worshipped the same God. This was their common thread—Christianity, Judaism, and Islam. This form of inclusivism said that Abrahamic religions sprouted from the same seed, which sought out a meaning to the complexities of life. The Vatican admits that the doctrine, teaching, and rituals of other monotheistic religions may differ from their own, but the guidelines on how to live a good life are universal and timeless—something that transcends denomination.

2. Abu-Nimer et al., *Unity in Diversity*, 10–19.

3. Abu-Nimer et al., *Unity in Diversity*, 19.

4. Bongiovanni, Interview.

Nostra Aetate encourages Christians to witness for themselves the "spiritual and moral truths"[5] evident in many non-Christian societies and traditions. In paragraph 3 of the decree, the most interesting information is revealed on how the church wants to guide the future relationship of Christians and Muslims. The tenets of Islam are extolled, such as their fasting, love of prayer, charity, and consideration for the poor:

> "The Church has also a high regard for the Muslims. They worship God, who is one, living and subsistent, merciful and almighty, the Creator of heaven and earth, [1] who has also spoken to men (. . .) Although not acknowledging him as God, they worship Jesus as a prophet, his virgin Mother they also honor (. . .) For this reason, they highly esteem an upright life and worship God, especially by way of prayer, alms deeds and fasting."[6]

The powerful, bordering on radical, inclusive message at the heart of this decree was not lost on the young Fr. Paolo. It would become the most illuminating of beacons for him, as he set his moral compass toward his spiritual journey to the heart of Islam and Syria. Nobody was more enthusiastic about the principles endorsed by the decree than Fr. Paolo, for Catholics could now be agents of reconciliation with the blessing of the hierarchy, free to "wash the feet of those perceived to be one's enemies."[7]

No wonder religious humanists, like Fr. Paolo and the like-minded nuns and monks of Al-Khalil, would take up the mantle of *Nostra Aetate*. It was a short document, but its brief outline was the rough sketch of a concept that would later be taken on and developed by various interreligious visionaries over the coming decades, some even going so far as to push the boundaries of conventional religious practice by advocating a synthesis of cross-religious rituals. IFD could be a tool for mediation between religions that might assuage a painful shared history. Often words

5. Second Vatican Council, "Nostra Aetate," 1965.

6. Second Vatican Council, "Nostra Aetate," 1965.

7. O'Malley SJ, *The Legacy of Vatican II*, 11.

like 'Crusade' or 'Jihad' still fill the air with anxiety and tension.[8] Leaders with vision were needed who could unite people in their communal heritage and, in the process, transcend inflexible doctrine, and entrenched historical mistrust.

Rome's View on IFD

To supplement *Nostra Aetate*, The Pontifical Council of the Vatican published guidelines[9] on different modes of Interfaith Dialogue that it identifies as being helpful for practitioners. It looks at four of the main modes:

> 1) The Dialogue of Life in which people of different faiths get to know each other through living together or engaging in daily routines and interactions.
>
> 2) The Dialogue of Words or practical cooperation, where people cooperate together on a community-specific project with a defined goal that can benefit everyone involved.
>
> 3) The Dialogue of Experts, which in contrast to the grassroots and egalitarian experience of the first two modes of dialogue, stresses the importance of experts from the religious hierarchy or academia comparing and contrast theological and ritualistic differences between faiths.
>
> 4) The Dialogue of Believers, where members of the joint congregations come together to share their experiences of spirituality, prayer etc.

As we will come to understand, the Interfaith Dialogue that was being carried out in Mar Musa under the tutelage of Fr. Paolo and his team encompassed, to some degree, all of these different modes. That said, it also had distinctly Syrian traits that were a direct result of the religious, social, and political context in which the dialogue was taking place.

8. Abu-Nimer et al., *Unity in Diversity,* 22.

9. Episcopal Commission, "A Church in Dialogue."

The First Stirrings of Interfaith
Dialogue (IFD) in Syria

In Arabic, the term for dialogue is *hiwar*, which can be interpreted as swapping opinions in conversation. Interfaith Dialogue in Syria is usually referred to as *al-hiwar bayn al-adyan*, which literally translates as "the dialogue between the religions."[10] The Ba'athists have been in power in Syria since the 1960s, controlling much of the religious landscape—including dialogue efforts. Prof. Szanto, expert on IFD in Syria and attendee at IFD seminars in Mar Musa, insists that IFD as an official practice helped to provide the Alawite regime with a form of religious legitimacy.[11]

The first and most prominent Syrian religious leader to take part in IFD efforts from the 1970s onwards was the late Grand Mufti Ahmad Kuftaro. This was something of a coup for the regime as Kuftaro was an esteemed and well-respected Sunni cleric and his initiatives in IFD provided the Ba'athists with credibility. According to Prof. Szanto, regime restrictions on IFD were eased a little in the nineties, and by 2006 major participants included Salah ad-Dīn Kuftaru, the Grand Mufti's son; Dr. al-Habash, a parliamentarian and Ahmad Kuftaru's protégé; Fr. Elias Zahlawī, a Damascene Catholic priest; and Fr. Paolo Dall'Oglio.[12]

Prof. Szanto identified striking differences between Muslim and Christian approaches to dialogue, both in methods and aims, which lead to miscommunication. Muslims sheikhs strove for unity in society by teaching people virtues in the struggle against immorality, injustice, and atheism, yet they tended to avoid demystifying other religions and failed to teach religious differences; on the other side, Christian clerics espoused love as being paramount and aimed to bolster tolerance by encouraging affection and awareness of others. Unfortunately, most IFD efforts within Syria were primarily aimed at strengthening domestic ties and demonstrating Syrian unity. This followed the Ba'athist party line of promoting

10. Szanto, "Inter-Religious Dialogue in Syria," 1.
11. Szanto, "Inter-Religious Dialogue in Syria," 2.
12. Szanto, "Inter-Religious Dialogue in Syria," 2.

Arab nationalism and the thin veneer of a united front, rather than attempting to achieve actual mutual understanding among the religiously diverse communities of the country.

Kuftaru once exclaimed that he was "'against dialogue with Syrian Christians' and argued that in Syria, Muslims and Christians were 'beyond dialogue.'"[13] On another occasion, when asked about a purely Syrian Interfaith Dialogue initiative, he said, "we will not convince and convert each other, so there is no point in dialogue."[14] According to Prof. Szanto, Kuftaru believed the soul of IFD was "maintaining communal etiquette."[15] Appearance was valued over substance.

In contrast, Fr. Paolo had a different view when Prof. Szanto interviewed him back in August 2006. He thought that spirituality and morality were intrinsically connected to one's social and political well-being, "the link can be summarized by the concept of 'ta'arruf,' or 'getting to know each other.'"[16] Hospitality and ecumenical worship, a redefinition of the parameters of religious friendship, were the most important things for the Italian at the helm in Mar Musa.

Fr. Paolo's progressive IFD ethos struck a chord with Muslim peers also. During one notable interfaith conference in Mar Musa in 2006, a prominent Muslim cleric, contrary to the views of Kuftaru, radically underscored Fr. Paolo's sentiment by proclaiming that unconditional love for all people—irrespective of their sins and failings—can have a transformative impact on Christian-Muslim relations in eliminating prejudice and ignorance.[17] In this type of IFD, there was no retrospective glancing back at the injustices of the past, whether it be the crusades or foreign colonization; instead, the Al-Khalil philosophy was forward-looking. Historical and political differences needed to be swept aside, leaving the path ahead clear for discussion and engagement.

13. Szanto, "Inter-Religious Dialogue in Syria," 5.

14. Szanto, "Inter-Religious Dialogue in Syria," 9.

15. Szanto, Interview.

16. Szanto, "Inter-Religious Dialogue in Syria," 10.

17. Szanto, Interview.

Chapter 3: **Al-Khalil's Hospitality**

Oases in the Desert

Daily Life in Mar Musa Monastery

A fine flock of 103 goats ambled jauntily around the rocky surrounds of Mar Musa until 2012, when the threat of war made keeping the animals impractical. Until then, they had to be tended to every morning—religiously. In the first years, they stayed under the rooms in the monastery, snuggling for warmth in the cold winter desert nights. Guests and workers in bed directly above them had the full sensory farmstead experience.

Members of the religious Community would wake up in the early hours to milk them. Afterwards, they would be released into the surrounding mountains to explore and nibble whatever vegetation they could find. You could often see them rambling about on their promontory in the clouds above you, expertly navigating the craggy rocks. Their strong rich milk would be boiled in the dairy section of the monastery, the creamy bounty magically transformed through an alchemy of acids into mouth-watering cheeses and yogurts that monks, nuns, guests, and workers, all greedily devoured.

During the early-morning cheese-making process, a large enticing pot of strong black coffee would bubble away on the stove triumphantly, its rich unmistakable aroma infusing the simple room, teasing the nostrils of those gathered, before being poured ceremoniously into small glasses. This was a time to savor, each person present waiting patiently for the large vat of goat's milk to boil. There was the stir of activity, boisterous chat, bleary-eyed arguments, and teasing discussion, others were lost in thought or listening to the radio, tuning their ears into what was happening in that distant world outside of their world. A foreign and often confusing reality that was piped into their sealed communal space.

The monk Boutros was in charge of cheese production. He was Syrian Orthodox from Hassakeh and a big football fan. His local team were *Al Jezira,* not to be confused with the Qatari television station. He had studied to be a lawyer but felt deep unease in the city so had fled its clutches and came to the monastery and the desert that encases it in 1996. He was given money and chased away unceremoniously by Fr. Paolo. The howl of the impatient Italian should have been enough to put anyone off a second attempt—anyone except Boutros! He pig-headedly refused the indignity of this initial rejection, returning once again, only to hear the Italian yell incredulously, "I kicked you out and you are back!?" But such stubbornness may have perversely appealed to Fr. Paolo's own nature, and he eventually agreed to try him out for a week . . . and Boutros is still there!

Boutros says, "When I was young, I asked, are Christians and Muslims different? Other monasteries I was at, didn't help answer that question. Then I came here and felt at peace. I attended many Interfaith Dialogue conferences and had animated discussions with Paolo. I read books on Islam and Sufism. I've reached a conclusion that I believe in deeply: a person is a person."[1]

Deir Mar Musa did not follow a typical monastic rule and had only two prayer meetings a day, but there was a specific routine. Morning prayers, inspired by passages from the bible or hymns would usually begin at 07:30. A hymn started and then candles were lit. Prayer would be initiated after reciting Holy, Holy, Holy! and then Fr. Paolo often taught for everyone present, taking a different Catholic article day to day, focusing on it for up to one hour. Prayers would conclude at 09:30 and a late breakfast was served. Afterwards everyone would work,

1. Fedda, *A Tale of Two Syrias.* 20:35–21:05.

going about their own individual tasks and responsibilities until mid-afternoon—tending the garden, cleaning, sweeping, washing, drying.

When the workers, volunteers, and clergy finished their chores, they would share lunch together. There would usually be some free time after 15:00 until sun down. In the summer and spring with the longer days, there were throngs of people arriving and plenty of activity about the place. Later at 19:30, they gathered for one hour of meditation. In the darkness, they would collectively chanted a hymn for the light, say the Our Father and the Hail Mary, and ask for mercy. There they would stay until 20:30 in complete silence in the Sufi-style of meditation.

Mass was celebrated at 08:00 on Sundays. The ceremony would depend on how many guests there were and the languages they spoke—for the homily particularly. It would usually be translated for anyone who needed it. The Community were very conscious of guests' needs and accommodated them whenever possible. There were bibles in many languages too—Japanese, Korean, Polish, etc. Afterwards, if anyone wanted to add something that was on their mind, they had the opportunity. It was open and interactive in the morning, whereas in the evening it was more about personal reflection and spiritual awareness. Then, after evening mass, there would be supper. Bed times varied as during the summer the youth would stay up later, maybe even after midnight—singing, talking, laughing.

Sadly, for the last few years during wartime, no one has been coming anymore to Mar Musa. The monks and nuns who decided to stay have had lots of time for work and prayer. Recently this is already changing and people are starting to reappear, like hardy flowers breaking through the last snows to receive the first rays of a spring sun.

Mar Musa's Interfaith Dialogue:
A Way of Life.

Fr. Paolo's philosophy permeated everyday life across Al-Khalil and his base in Mar Musa. It was showcased through the annual IFD summer seminars, but it was also the more informal casual dialogue of daily life. The spontaneous cross-religious dialogue that occurred through the lived daily experiences of the rivers of volunteers, workers, teachers, and clergy who passed through the small monastery was genuine and unselfconscious, as was the surprise of guests who were welcomed into the bosom of the Community like long lost sons and daughters. Food and board were offered in return for small chores that needing doing around the site.

Friendship was one word that summed up the Interfaith Dialogue work of Al-Khalil; it was also a core pillar of the Community. This mirrored the Muslim view that elevated interfaith friendship to a position of prominence as described by the Qur'an; it is announced to Muslims that, among men, Christians will be the "nearest in friendship."[2]

In addition to its day-to-day commitment to dialogue, IFD in Mar Musa was made up of a variety of different approaches and tasks. Yes, there were annual religious events as well as cultural, agricultural, and environmental conferences of a more formal nature. The formal IFD seminars, organized annually since 2003, were just one piece of a larger framework of events. Sometimes there were dialogue sessions, community projects, spiritual retreats, horticultural/environmental/biodiversity workshops, 'Masir,'[3] manual labor, songs. It varied depending on the needs of the Community and the guests who were available to deliver talks.[4] Not all the seminars took place in Mar Musa either. One event was hosted by Mar Elian in Al-Qaryatayn in 2001. The Community were joined

2. Merad, *Christian Hermit*, Kindle Loc.552.

3. Long walks in the desert or countryside with a spiritual guide, primarily organized by Fr. Frans van der Lugt from Homs. (Interview, Bashir, February, 2018.)

4. Bashir, Interview.

by friends from across the Arab world—notably Egypt and Sudan. It was not a dialogue seminar per se, but was aimed at Christians living in Muslim majority countries.

There can be no analysis of IFD in Mar Musa without a discussion of the guiding pillars that fed the teachings of Fr. Paolo and his religious team. There is of course an overlap here with the Syriac monastic tradition and the work of de Foucauld. When the Community introduced themselves, they said that they were monks and nuns, men and women, brothers and sisters, sinners and the forgiven, invited to the desert by the LORD.[5] Fr. Paolo would refer to them as "Disciples of Jesus living in a Muslim context."[6]

The 3 guiding tenets of the Community were:

- Spirituality: a focus on the absolute value of the spiritual life with a devotion to prayer and contemplation.

- Manual work: the importance of physical work was not based around production since the monastery never aimed to be self-sufficient. Instead, they worked for the value of work. Young people were also involved in this practice. They helped around the site, planting trees and making goats' cheese—both for the educational value and the mindfulness of such activities. These gestures of creation were calming and spiritually rewarding.

- Abrahamic hospitality: in each guest the nuns and monks of Mar Musa received God and in the faces of their guests they saw the face of Jesus. Each guest had various needs. Some may have come out of curiosity, a spiritual quest, etc. The fostering of mutual understanding was vital, as was building bridges between communities.

IFD work in Al-Khalil encompassed each of the aforementioned pillars in its framework. Outside of the more formal yearly seminars, it was indeed a lifestyle. Interfaith Dialogue, as an act, was not just a single event reserved for a particular week each

5. Bashir, Interview.
6. Dall'Oglio, *Innamorato dell'Islam*, 44.

year—it was ongoing. All who visited Mar Musa were included in IFD, regardless of whether they had planned their visits or were merely passing through—irrespective of their religious affiliation, the organizations they represented, or their nationality.

Their philosophy regarding manual work was particularly striking as it becomes fused with the spiritual. Work was prayer and both could be seamlessly interchanged as manual work need not always be physical. It could be simple things such as classifying books in the library, working on the computer, etc.

They aspired to be completely self-sufficient but it was unrealistic considering the numbers of visitors they hosted. More important was the *value* of the work for the monks, nuns, and their guests. It developed them—their personalities, their minds. It also provided a bulwark against dark thoughts and moods. There was a famous slogan of St. Benedict: *ora et labora*—prayer and work. It was a partnership between men and God. Manual work was a gesture of this partnership as they entered a dialogue with the physical material world.[7] Fr. Paolo saw physical work as a way of elevating manual labor to a spiritual level that was on a par with a communion with God; a form of prayer.

Guests and Participants

It is important to reiterate that Interfaith Dialogue in Mar Musa was both formal—occasional planned seminars and conferences, and informal—ongoing and sustained. This is evident by the continuous flow of guests who dropped in to sample the Community's renowned hospitality—a hearty welcome, warm meal, and soft(ish) bed if so required. In fact, hospitality was part of the fabric of the Community since its very inception in 1991, with the more formal planned IFD seminars coming over a decade later.

There was a ceaseless wave of guests to Mar Musa. Unlike the yearly Interfaith Dialogue conferences, no invitation was necessary to visit. The impromptu visits, the dinners, the talk,

7. Bashir, Interview.

the friendship-building, the welcome—it all seemed spontaneous and effortless and, most importantly, permanent. Author Robert Tewdwr Moss gives a humorous account of the eclectic nature of those who visited Mar Musa to avail of the famous welcome, many of them dropping by and staying the night on an impulse:

> "Our party for dinner that evening consisted of one Jesuit, one Syrian Catholic, one Syrian Orthodox, one Moslem, one Armenian Christian, one Armenian Moslem, one French Catholic, one Algerian-French Moslem, one Welsh Calvinist-turned-pantheist, and one Agnostic. The Zen Buddhists or Shinto-ites (. . .) had left after the service."[8]

Not everyone agreed with Fr. Paolo about the increasing number of backpackers descending on Mar Musa from early spring each year. It was hard work accommodating them all. Elena, an Italian and the first female member of the monastery, felt she had a vocation for dialogue, however she disagreed with Fr. Paolo about how to go about it—particularly regarding the tourists and backpackers who were arriving at the site. Prof. Loosley explains that "There was some disagreement about the unlimited hospitality on offer at the monastery. She [Sister Elena] insisted that there needed to be a more manageable way of dealing with such numbers. Paolo disagreed, saying that people could come unannounced at any time."[9] This was one of the factors that influenced her decision to leave in 2001. She now continues her vocation in Italy working with refugee communities.

Fr. Paolo insisted there could be no compromise on the key pillar of Al-Khalil—hospitality. They had to nurture this atmosphere of acceptance through their actions, words, and sentiments. According to Fr Paolo, it was their collective mission to bring people closer together and unite. Capping visitor numbers or not being unequivocal in their offer of charity and welcome was simply unconscionable.

8. Moss, *Cleopatra's Wedding Present*, 55.

9. Loosley, Interview.

The formal interfaith seminars, which had been organized annually in Mar Musa since 2003, had a mix of participants and it is worth examining how they were chosen. Often in IFD in the Middle East, the clergy and elite members of society were exclusively involved. In Mar Musa, it was more egalitarian in its approach. Lots of people participated—local clergy, monks, academics, nuns, Orthodox Christians, Catholics, laypeople, women. In addition, young people from all sides were also attending the discussions. Secular and lay participants would occasionally outnumber those from religious institutions in organized formal IFD sessions in Mar Musa, but the mix was often evenly split.[10]

The system of invitation was also based on a referral process. People who had been invited could then invite friends, friends of friends etc. In some countries in the Middle East, it is clear that IFD struggles to attract qualified and respected Muslim religious figures. However, in Mar Musa, this was not an issue. Their aim was to include a representative cross-section of society. They always had important religious figures and laypeople—together. Imams and religious people were invited and they often brought their friends with them. You could find Christian bishops and Muslim imams side by side, along with Kurdish, Sunni, Shia, Alawite. Status was not the most important thing for the Community when considering invitations.[11]

When lay members of the local community were invited, they would then bring friends along with them. This was on a purely voluntary basis and no pressure was applied. Of course no one was forced to come. They wanted people to attend who *wanted* to be there.[12]

Those who attended formal seminars had been formally invited and talks were organized thematically. Prominent figures would come prepared to talk on their topic of interest. It was more theoretical, theological, intellectual. It was about faith, religious practices, etc. Others were not convinced about the merit of the

10. Bashir, Interview.
11. Bashir, Interview.
12. Bashir, Interview.

formal seminars. Prof. Edith Szanto, who attended one of the events, said that it was mostly government-chosen religious figures who led the formal seminars:

> "I attended a formal IFD seminar in Mar Musa in 2006. The reason I remember is that my parents were there. Sitting beside them was one of the funders from Germany. He kept asking them comically, 'when is it over, when is it over?' There were some foreigners, some locals. I didn't think they attracted that many secular people. They were preaching to the choir anyway. There were women and young people but it was more about appearance. There were religious government figures in attendance like Kuftaru and his son and others (. . .) Key speakers in their fields came for one or two talks and then left. They were waiting for the clock to run down. In formal IFD sessions, the situation didn't lend itself to talking about social issues. The speakers were state-affiliated and so it was a theatrical performance with little substance behind it."[13]

For Fr. Paolo though, formal IFD still had a purpose. It provided an opportunity for the Community to showcase and disseminate their message more widely among their religious peers.

The informal dialogue of daily life—the beating heart of the Community's core mission of hospitality—moved away from the more overt religious elements of formal sessions. Religious doctrine was in the background, choosing instead to focus on manual labor, food preparation/production, etc. While working or building, Christians and Muslims would discuss things and it was a chance to open up and participate in a form of reciprocal learning. In daily life, this was also a way to naturally approach the Muslim side and bond during small menial tasks. Whereas, the formal seminars were a concentrated effort to do things and complete objectives, the casual dialogue of daily life was natural, unselfconscious, and as equally effective at fostering friendship and cross-community communication.

13. Szanto, Interview.

The many guests of Mar Musa throughout the years—locals and backpackers alike—came from a broad cross-section of society. This open door policy, which Fr Paolo had insisted upon, worked in the monastery's favor in terms of how the Community were perceived. Laypeople were at ease in this relaxed and natural setting as it stressed a more familiar social context. It also offered locals the chance to meet people from other countries, and vice versa, giving them all a unique occasion to temporarily immerse themselves in a different culture.

Youth and Women

The inclusion of women and young people from the local community in formal and informal dialogue was of pivotal importance in reiterating the non-hierarchical and inclusive message at the heart of Mar Musa and Al-Khalil—a message that emphasized openness and tolerance. Fr. Paolo was conscious that dialogue bears most fruit when it is bottom-up in its approach, when all sectors of society—especially youth and women—actively participate in it. Young people constitute one of the most important elements of any society as they are representative of what the country will aspire to and the foundations on which the future is built.

The Community knew what was at stake in the religiously diverse maelstrom of Assad's Syria. Social inclusion, not exclusion, was their motivating force. The rivers of young people—local and foreign—came with a huge thirst to discover God and the absolute. It was a unique opportunity for locals to meet other people, speak some English, and talk about their shared experiences.[14]

Across other Al-Khalil monasteries this ethos is still ongoing. Including children in the services and programs is a priority for Fr. Jens, who now heads Deir Maryam al-Adhra in Sulaymaniyah, Iraq. He talks about how they encourage the youth to participate in inter-religious activities there. During mass the children are involved in the ceremony, each of them having a little job to do, actively lighting

14. Bashir, Interview.

candles, singing, chanting etc. They are a very open Community and are always adapting to their surroundings.[15]

On other occasions, the team in Deir Maryam would find young people who were already engaged in their respective communities and try to organize various trips with them. They visit sites of commemoration together, like the memorial in Halabja.[16] From time to time students of religion—both Christian and Muslim—would come by Fr. Jens' office and have a question and answer session. "Sometimes religion students would drop by and have discussions with us," Fr. Jens explains. "I very much enjoyed these visits, for it was an opportunity to be open and explain things. Interesting questions were always asked and the young people seemed curious and got a lot out of it."[17] It was a small step towards making the other side less mysterious, more human.

The role of women in Mar Musa was also a key component in its experience of dialogue. Women could stay in the Catholic monastery too, however, it was not unique in Middle Eastern terms as the Syrian Orthodox also maintain dual housing for both women and men. Mar Musa reverted to an older more idiosyncratic model of monasticism that Catholicism had rejected in the middle ages. This was a marked and progressive move away from traditional monastic doctrine regarding cohabitation between the sexes.

It all started in 1993 when Elena arrived at the monastery with a letter from the Italian Arch Bishop of Milan requesting that she be allowed stay. Until that point Fr. Paolo had not thought about a female presence in Mar Musa. A female quarters was then developed and slowly this gradually became more and more popular.[18]

Fr Paolo, while traditional in many respects, strongly believed in equality. Based on respect and friendship, we were all equal before God. The nuns of Mar Musa even wore male clothing. Their

---

15. Petzold, Interview.

16. The Halabja Chemical Attack took place in the town in March 1988 on the mostly civilian Kurdish population and was carried out by the Iraqi forces of Saddam Hussein. (Yildiz, *The Kurds in Iraq*, 27.)

17. Petzold, Interview.

18. Petzold, Interview.

unisex attire looked exactly like that of their male counterparts.[19] Life at the monastery involved a daily relationship with women. They were all aware of the emotional and sexual possibilities that exist between men and women. The Community had all made a vow of chastity, but they tried not to ignore that integral part of their humanity. Humanity and sexuality were always there, never hidden, and they tried to deal with these challenges. A model of the male/female relationship not based on sex was forged.[20]

Even though women had played a key role in the renovation and development of the monastery, the rather common-sense idea of cohabitation did not go down well with the hierarchy and local Patriach Daoud. Despite such opposition, Fr. Paolo was steadfast and persevered, after all, many women had contributed to the restoration of the frescos—only one man had taken part in this undertaking. "Hard physical labor was often undertaken by women," Fr. Jens recalls. "In light of this, Fr. Paolo thought it really should be a Community of *both* men and women. After all, we were in the desert, if women came to seek shelter, better to have other women there to look after them."[21]

Patriach Daoud strongly wanted separation between the sexes in the complex. Two clearly defined living areas. At the beginning, the monks were on the second floor and the nuns on the first. Later the nuns stayed in the old part of the monastery and the monks moved to the newer area. The work, the prayer, and all the activities were organized together. It felt natural and there were few issues.[22]

The monks and nuns would also go to Damascus and invite females to the monastery. Sometimes the imams brought their wives, or teachers would bring fellow female teachers from their schools, etc. In this way, a rich and diverse network was created

19. Szanto, Interview.
20. Bashir, Interview.
21. Petzold, Interview.
22. Petzold, Interview.

down through the years. They would willingly come to share and participate.[23]

The progressive co-habitation stance undertaken in Mar Musa, meant that the Community became the focus of a lot of spiteful gossip, but there were no salacious facts to feed the rumor mill. "It was a source of honor that the Community mixed daily with the opposite sex," states Prof. Loosley. "They openly acknowledged that it was often difficult, but it was more important to have equitable, platonic relationships."[24] In fact, the lack of scandal was a cause for dismay in the eyes of many who disliked Fr. Paolo and the Community.

Interfaith Dialogue in Practice

Formal IFD in Mar Musa consisted of a mix of cognitive dialogue (comparing theological and religious traditions, learning about other faiths) and affective dialogue (socially-focused, with an eye on building relationships through shared stories from people's lives).[25] Admittedly, the more cognitive element took priority. Formal seminars had a theological/theoretical focus but there was an overlap as it was usually connected to society and social practices in some way.[26]

The type of dialogue that characterized formal IFD sessions in Mar Musa was linked with the demographic of the participants. There was a reasonable mix of religious and secular participants, clergy and lay people. Subsequently, the programs in Mar Musa, to some extent, overcame one of the more challenging aspects of making formal dialogue less hierarchical. A real attempt to subvert traditional Christian-Muslim dialogue in formal IFD, from the top-down-focused approach prevalent throughout much of the region, was admirable. Topics for dialogue varied, but at times

23. Bashir, Interview.
24. Loosely, Interview.
25. Abu-Nimer et al., *Unity in Diversity,* 16.
26. Bashir, Interview.

there was an unconscious mixing of both secular and religious strands, with no clear dividing line.

Religion for Fr. Paolo was that which united and differentiated us, simultaneously. We share religious experiences, we share the very core of our faith with others. In Mar Musa, the focus was on religious-based dialogue but not exclusively. Admittedly, there was often more of a focus on religious issues, but it is hard to speak of religion without speaking about life.[27]

This suggests a more fluid and malleable interpretation of secular and religious topics with regard to IFD in the monastery. There is an overlap; one is not mutually exclusive of the other. However, the attendance of the Syrian state security services at formal IFD sessions undoubtedly influenced the content of discussions and the choice of topics on the table.

Mar Musa's more informal dialogue of daily life offered a non-judgmental mutual space for people to get to know each other away from the rigidity of more formal seminars and the presence of the state security services. Many visitors and guests were Muslims who had a unique chance to come and socialize with Christians; both could explain their rituals, see each other pray, tell stories about their life and education together, read the Qur'an and discuss it afterwards. A safe place where both sides could learn from each other's beliefs—directly from the source. The everyday life of the monastery was where you could catch a real glimpse of how Christian faith could be incorporated into a Muslim reality.[28]

There was a crucial societal process being enacted in Mar Musa: the demystification and humanization of the religious *other*. Ignorance is our enemy, for when we ignore people, we fear them. Love destroys fear and pushes you to know the *other*. Familiarity and knowledge breed love therefore humanization is an important term. Humanization is another form of holiness.[29]

Prof. Bongiovanni talks of the quintessentially Mar Musa experience:

27. Bashir, Interview.
28. Bashir, Interview.
29. Bashir, Interview.

"Mar Musa was a sort of sharing and common hospitality program between Muslims and Christians. I think it was special. His [Fr. Paolo's] idea was an open place, where people could share, meet, talk, eat—together. In that sense, it was very unique. Religious dialogue encourages a practical friendship and sharing. People who go there are very touched by the experience. That is the importance and the miracle of dialogue. It can change people and give us a better understanding of our faith in the presence of the *other*."[30]

Fr. Jens takes another approach as to how the notion of engagement with the religious *other* is important, while also respecting the idea that the *other* should remain distinct, keeping its uniqueness. He says:

"I don't know if I want to demystify anything. I am a priest and in the business of mystifying! Anyway, now in the twenty-first century you are no longer able to be ignorant of the *other*. We are always together with them. How can we ignore them? Here, in Deir Maryam, we aim to start with curiosity. This is the bedrock. What is so special in the Middle East? Respecting each other. Having a shared cultural life."[31]

This is confirmed by Fr. Paolo's own theological musings on the nature of his work. Religious differences should not be tamed or assimilated, but rather, we should fall in love with the very essence of *otherness*.[32] This was classic Mar Musa—living together and respecting each other was indeed possible.[33]

Storytelling

Storytelling, a form of affective dialogue, was another fruitful way to move away from a more religious-centered approach which

30. Bongiovanni, Interview.
31. Petzold, Interview.
32. Dall'Oglio, *Innamorato dell'Islam,* 46.
33. Bashir, Interview

compares and contrasts religious doctrine, instead approaching IFD from a more social and personal angle.[34] This was successfully utilized in Mar Musa, with the monks and nuns encouraging participants to recount their own personal narratives, helping them feel at ease. They talked and shared their stories, discussing things in smaller groups where everyone had a voice.[35]

Usually this would be initiated by a monk or nun telling one of their own stories as an ice-breaker. Discussing life, jobs, and the daily challenges faced in Syrian society at the time, was an effective way to bridge the divide between the religious and the secular. Social issues were discussed, but usually within a religious context. If a sister arrived, she would talk about her school and talk about classes, teaching, books, exercises, the syllabus, class programs, etc.[36]

Fr. Paolo used to tell his own personal stories at these sessions—to get things started. It is also recounted in his book *Innamorato dell'Islam, credente in Gesù [Lover of Islam: Believer in Jesus]*. He tells us of stopping in Bosra, an ancient city founded by the Romans. In the evening, exhausted after travelling all day, he finds a mosque. On entering the courtyard, two young men welcome him and they start talking about religion. After a few short exchanges, he tells them, "I'm dirty after a day's traveling. I would like to express my respect for the mosque, the house of God, by performing the ablutions." On hearing this, they give him a pitcher of water and he goes to the bathroom for a brief wash.

When he comes back, they sit together on the stone benches facing each other and the same men teach him the words and gestures of ritual cleansing for Muslims. When the time comes for the evening prayer, the men and children fill the mosque, asking that he join them in prayer.[37] The young Jesuit never forgot this day. The experience stayed long in his memory for the simple kindness and generosity shown towards him—a person of different faith. His personal experience of inclusiveness and acceptance within

34. Abu-Nimer et al., *Unity in Diversity*, 16.

35. Bashir, Interview.

36. Bashir, Interview.

37. Dall'Oglio, *Innamorato dell'Islam*, 21–22.

Islam, his hard-wired sense of double-belonging, can be traced to this moment—almost half a decade before he rediscovered Mar Musa. It was 1978, and a defining moment in the Italian's spiritual and theological journey.

Prayer and Spirituality

Undertaking prayer in such a religiously pluralist backdrop had its challenges. Questions were raised as to how to negotiate that most sensitive and personal ritual between the creeds in a shared religious area like Mar Musa. Fr. Paolo once invited Muslim guests to participate in reciting the LORD's Prayer in the small chapel. One Muslim visitor, Shady Hamadi, notes that the Community aspired to make the act of prayer a common, shared, and inclusive ritual for all who passed through. He states, "Then we went to see Fr. Paolo and we entered the little chapel. We said the LORD's Prayer. This prayer is neutral, all religions can say it and it seemed right for us then."[38] If some of the Muslims weren't familiar with the prayer, they could also participate in shared Prayers of the Faithful during mass in the chapel.

There would be a meditation time together and then a mass where Muslims were welcome to come and join the congregation in Mar Musa's chapel. During the Prayers of the Faithful, an open space became available where anyone could pray for anything they wanted. When Muslims prayed, the monks and nuns would stay behind and participate spiritually with them.[39]

That spiritual element was harnessed effectively as a means of bringing people closer, like partaking in shared silences as a substitute for prayer. There is some consensus in IFD circles that one means of steering clear of interfaith misunderstandings is to avoid interfaith prayer altogether, and instead opt for a common, shared

38. Hamadi, Interview.
39. Bashir, Interview.

silence between groups.[40] This was a neutral compromise to navigate the delicate and personal space of interreligious prayer.

In Mar Musa, these silences went further than the mere absence of sound as a medium to worship; they would blend elements of Sufi mysticism with trance-like chanting or music, which worked as a common link between the tribes. Communal prayer sessions would be set up through the medium of meditation, music, and chanting etc. Sufi poetry uses the metaphor that flowers are different in smell and appearance—but irrigated by the same water. The monastic life is interlinked with Sufism due to its mystical aspirations.[41]

In these ways, people from both sides could partake in a communal meditative exercise. Sufism stresses the spiritual element of communion with God through chanting and music. Fr. Jens says:

> "This chanting facilitates mindfulness and a concentration only on the body and the essential. You try to get your mind in-line with your heart. Chanting is one means of achieving this. Like running. When you run, you are in total harmony with your body and almost in a trance, but you also need to be alert and aware. It's like an in-between state. A different kind of consciousness."[42]

It was a force that united those present, regardless of faith, with God. A quality that Sufism shared with the Christian monastic tradition, as practiced by de Foucauld and Fr. Paolo, was its emphasis on the solitary life and its deep connection between the spiritual and the divine.

The Community would also meld this spiritual leaning with more theological dialogue by comparing and contrasting rituals or sections of scripture. Sometimes after eating, they created these chanting circles—*Zikr*—meaning memory of Allah. They would all pray together and everyone would sing their songs or chant. There would be musical instruments like flutes etc. Occasionally they would create a small musical phrase and repeat it for ten minutes

40. Abu-Nimer et al., *Unity in Diversity*, 25.

41. Bashir, Interview.

42. Petzold, Interview.

like a form of meditative chanting. Sufi texts would be chosen, and a specific phrase would be given a simple melody. The musicians would then repeat it polyphonically. Through this, they could create simple chants that would be hypnotic and meditative—lasting for up to thirty minutes.[43] These were yet more examples of the progressive religious acts being undertaken in Mar Musa and the synthesizing of cross-religious practices. The mystical component of Sufism was harnessed in the monastery as a spiritual extension between Islam and Christianity.

Muslims occasionally prayed in the small church in Mar Musa. Since it was a Catholic monastery, the church always remained prominent, but Fr. Paolo and his team had some rather radical ideas about spaces of shared worship that could be multi-denomination in character.

Once there was a large group of people from a wide array of different religions. They wanted to pray, so Fr. Paolo set them an intriguing task: they had to come up with an idea for a shared place of worship, a space that would be inclusive for everyone present. The religious Community were always exploring how they could express worship in a pluralist sense. They had this idea of a chapel/mosque and a third non-denominational area— one complex, with a courtyard that connected them, and rooms leading off into the various chambers. It was to be located below Mar Musa in the valley. "It was already in the architectural phase as we had organized a brainstorming session with young architects from all over the world," Fr. Jens states. "It would have been called a 'spiritual oasis.'"[44]

War came to Syria soon after and curtailed their ambitious plans. However, Prof. Szanto is not entirely convinced by this rather unconventional idea, seeing it as a step too far for the Muslim side. "Their planned spiritual oasis could have been tricky. A prayer space is ok but a mosque is a different matter," she states. "Muslims would have seen it as too much of a compromise. It's one thing coming

43. Bashir, Interview.
44. Petzold, Interview.

into a Christian space to pray, but quite another when Christians actually create your holy space. It's not mainstream."[45]

One event resonated particularly evocatively in its poignant simplicity. They were starting the evening prayer—the LORD's Prayer—but they were taking long breaths between each sentence. Pausing. There was silence in between the lines. It was very slow, in time with the rhythm of the heart and one's respiration. The Muslim groups also happened to be praying at this time outside in the tent and reciting the Tabor—repeating the phrase *Allāhu Akbar*. It was as if both prayers were fused. It was a deeply spiritual experience for those present.[46] There was a simple raw power in that hypnotic call and response between both chants. It was a sublime shared spiritual experience that transcended religious difference.

Shared Religious Festivals and Celebrations

Another pillar of IFD is shared interreligious ceremonies or festival periods. Such events were popular in Lebanon and Jordan, for example, during Ramadan. Iftar, the meal usually enjoyed after sunset during the Muslim month of fasting, is also celebrated in Egypt with the participation of local Christians.[47]

Christian religious festivals had a unique flavor in Mar Musa. For Christmas and Easter, there were always some young Muslims present. The staff of Mar Musa were a mix of Christians and Muslims together.[48] Initially, it appears as though there was no concerted effort to involve the local Muslim community in Christian religious feasts, apart from the staff of the monastery who had to be there anyway. Locals in the villages near the monastery would all work together—Christians and Muslims—to decorate the

---

45. Szanto, Interview.

46. Bashir, Interview.

47. Abu-Nimer et al., *Unity in Diversity*, 161.

48. Bashir, Interview.

entrances to their houses, both for Christmas or for the start of Muslim religious holidays. Everyone would rejoice together.

It becomes more interesting when the Muslim fasting month of Ramadan is mentioned. For Fr. Paolo, Ramadan was another form of Christian Lent. It was the perfect opportunity to have a shared experience—Muslims and Christians—by communion with God through fasting. He hoped that they would celebrate this period *together*, fusing the religious traditions of the area.[49]

This attitude was exemplified by the compassionate way that the monks and nuns of Mar Musa observed Ramadan out of respect for their Muslim staff. Many of the Community were observing the fast of Ramadan *with* the Muslim staff. They would wait with them until they finished work, until sundown, and then they would drink water with them before joining them for a meal. They fasted with them in solidarity. Some monks fasted for a few days, some for the whole month of Ramadan. It was not rigid or strict, however, the Community wanted to show support and be in full communion with their Muslims friends.[50]

This synthesizing of various spiritual interreligious practices was unusual and might have even been viewed by some as controversial. However, Fr. Paolo was a proponent of being aware of, and celebrating, that which we have in common with other religions—our shared practices, beliefs. On one occasion, the monks and nuns were praying and chanting in the church when a Muslim youth came in calmly but with purpose. He took one of the carpets which were available just inside the entrance, and he started to pray. It was very unselfconscious and there was something beautiful about it. They were praying all together. Everyone present was very touched, for he had felt comfortable enough to do this in their midst.[51]

Prof. Loosley, close friend of the Community, describes the time she spent in Mar Elian with Fr. Jacques Mourad and the

49. Bashir, Interview.
50. Bashir, Interview.
51. Bashir, Interview.

shared events involving both faiths that took place there. She describes the scene:

"Mar Elian was a shared shrine—Muslims and Christians worshipped there. Christians would bus in from as far away as Homs and Qurwani Muslims also venerated St. Julian. Thousands of pilgrims arrived every September for Eid Mar Elian (September 9). When the buses arrived, you didn't know who was Christian or Muslim. There would be communion, Muslims would wait, and then they would all eat and dance together."[52]

The sarcophagus of St. Julian would be covered with a Muslim shroud, but you could also find lit candles, rosary beads, and saints' images brought by people from both faiths.

Collaborative Interfaith Dialogue

Collaborative dialogue, which espouses community cooperation on a joint project with a practical purpose that benefits all sides of society, has seen success in some countries in the Middle East. It is also commonly known as dialogue through action.[53] These models are popular in Lebanon and involve people of different faiths undertaking a joint project together which highlights the universality of their shared experiences.[54] Members from both religious communities work together on a practical project towards an achievable shared goal. People get to know one another—a pivotal and often-overlooked form of relationship building. It might even be the starting point for all dialogue.

There were always ongoing projects in Al-Khalil that locals—both Muslims and Christians—cooperated on. They organized annual cultural and educational seminars and encouraged various religious groups to contribute. Once they had a session on music with Christian and Muslim groups playing together. There were

52. Loosley, Interview.
53. Abu-Nimer et al., *Unity in Diversity*, 160.
54. Abu-Nimer et al., *Unity in Diversity*, 26.

also seminars about biodiversity, as well as workshops on tree grafting, cheese making, recycling, raising awareness of the issue of desertification, littering and dumping, bee-keeping, animal husbandry etc.[55] This was a very modern and forward-thinking Community who were acutely aware of the importance of the natural world and its preservation.

Other ventures were more ambitious. One such project, which spanned a full ten years, involved all spectra of society—locals, monks and nuns, academics, and members of the government—working together to get permission for the area around Mar Musa to be designated a protected natural park. It was a resounding success as it was a collaboration between locals, the Mar Musa Community and experts, professors etc. Three ministries were involved: the Ministries of Tourism, the Environment and Agriculture. Mar Musa is a site of antiquities, so it was in everyone's interests to ensure it was protected. The local community and the monastery liaised with all three sides.[56] It demonstrated that people from disparate parts of society, and across various faiths, could work together successfully in achieving a goal that was in all their interests.

Joint Reconstruction/Development Projects

Mar Musa's ethos of cross-religious cooperation was put to the true test when the Syrian civil war started. The joint reconstruction projects that were undertaken at this time could be regarded as one of the real triumphs of IFD. As local housing and infrastructure lay in rubble after shelling, there was plenty of opportunity and a pressing need to undertake such ventures. Christians and Muslims were enthusiastic in the face of such challenges, for they now had a shared goal: tackle this problem together, get everyone back in their homes, and with a roof over their heads.

---

55. Bashir, Interview.
56. Bashir, Interview.

There was a battle in Nebek near Mar Musa in 2013 and many houses were flattened, leaving some local people destitute and homeless. Monks and locals, together, set about fixing the damage. They wanted people to stay. Up to seventy homes were repaired.[57] This was a resounding success and a vindication that the weight of their combined efforts could transcend traditionally inflexible religious, ethnic, and class boundaries.

Another opportunity came later, in Mar Musa's sister monastery of Mar Elian in Al-Qaryatayn, which had seen brutal fighting in its vicinity. Having learned from their first experience of cross-religious reconstruction work, this time tasks were carried out in a more efficient and highly coordinated fashion. Muslims and Christians worked together systematically, with interreligious assessment teams set up to weigh up the different needs of those who had suffered damage to their dwellings. Essential maintenance work was then undertaken on those homes. People were overwhelmed by the incredible generosity of those who gave limitless time and energy in the rebuilding efforts. Homes were rebuilt in Al-Qaryatayn and in the villages nearby (Mahin and Huwwarin). Up to one hundred homes were restored. It was emergency reconstruction for things like electricity, windows, water, sanitation, doors, etc.[58]

This kind of work undeniably crosses over into the dialogue of everyday life and might just be one of the most valuable and prized forms of IFD, helping, as it does, those united by misfortune. Bashir concurs:

> "This is one of the highest forms of IFD, as you transform theory into practice. You go to meet people. You help them for nothing. For the love of Christ. Not to convert them or to show yourself as being a good man. The majority of the people that were helped were Muslims. An assessment team was set up, consisting of Christians and Muslims together, to weigh up the needs of each family."[59]

57. Bashir, Interview.
58. Bashir, Interview.
59. Bashir, Interview.

These people who helped out were met as heroes in local homes, with food and love to repay them in kind for their generosity.

Not only did people come together on reconstruction projects, but during the initial fighting in the villages surrounding Mar Elian, many had been left homeless. In that interim period, the monastery offered refuge and a safe space away from the danger for many families. Up to fifty families (with more than a hundred children under twelve years old) were sheltering in the monastery for a period of three months during the fighting. They returned to ruined dwellings, but reconstruction teams helped them put their lives back together by fixing up the damage.[60]

This initiative is symbolically comparable to social projects in other Middle East countries, such as a tree-planting project which connected youth from various local Christian and Druze communities in Lebanon that previously had a troubled history.[61] IFD in this form can effectively channel the physical and social necessity for development projects that restructure and rehabilitate villages. People were connecting on a day-to-day level through these activities.

And so it was in Syria where the dialogue of life—a form of dialogue the Vatican also officially recognized—was prominent and had a very pressing practical need. Cooperation was casual, unselfconscious, and shared-goal driven. Losing your home is something everyone can empathize with, and these bonds of common compassion were unequivocally bolstered during these tough times. People came together selflessly to help their neighbors. Good neighborliness was a value close to Fr. Paolo too.

Unlike Fr. Jacques from Mar Elian, Fr. Paolo didn't have parishioners in the traditional sense of the word, yet he was fully committed to *all* the people from the local village of Nebek and its surrounds—regardless of denomination. They were all his parishioners. They were all equal in his eyes.

It seems that the people in these troubled areas did indeed love their neighbors at a time when the country was in the midst

60. Bashir, Interview.

61. Abu-Nimer et al., *Unity in Diversity*, 127.

of a violent sectarian period in its history. Tragically for Syria as a nation, suspicion and mistrust would soon supplant any feelings of togetherness.

Locations of the Al-Khalil Community across the Middle East

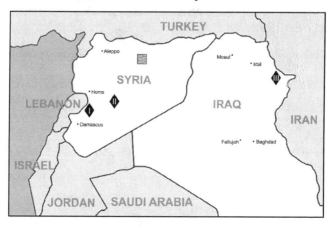

◆ Deir Mar Musa al-Habashi in Nebek (Syria)

◆ Deir Mar Elian in Al-Qaryatayn (Syria)

◆ Deir Maryam al-Adhra in Sulaymaniyah (Iraqi Kurdistan)

▨ Last known whereabouts of Fr. Paolo in Al-Raqqah (Syria)

Map by Adelina Krupski.

The monastery of Mar Musa al-Habashi
near Nebek, Syria. (photo O'Neill)

A bridge connects Mar Musa monastery to the other side of
the mountain. Fr. Paolo can be seen gesticulating at the top
in the common area. (photo O'Neill)

Participants gather during a formal IFD (Interfaith Dialogue) seminar
at Mar Musa in 2005. Fr. Paolo sits with his back to the camera
in black wearing a scarf. (photo unknown)

An imam and monk discuss event scheduling together
at an IFD seminar in 2005. (photo unknown)

Polish-Irish visitors in Mar Musa with Fr. Paolo (far right),
February 2011. (photo unknown)

Seminar during Eid Mar Elian in Al-Qaryatayn in 2001. On this occasion the Community of Al-Khalil were joined by friends from across the Arab world—notably Egypt and Sudan—as it was aimed at Christians living in Muslim-majority countries. From left, it shows Sister Houda, Fr. Jihad, Fr. Jacques, and many friends. At the front, smiling broadly, stands Fr. Paolo, to his left is Msgr Georges Kassab—the late Syrian Catholic Metropolitan of Homs, Hama and Nebek. (photo Loosley)

A shelf in the library of Deir Maryam al-Adhra, Sulaymaniyah, Iraq. (photo Tallova/Dohnany)

Fr. Jens Petzold relaxes in the courtyard of Deir Maryam,
Sulaymaniyah, Iraq, 2019. (photo Tallova/Dohnany)

Fr. Jacques Mourad shares a laugh with colleague Fr. Jens in Deir Maryam,
Sulaymaniyah, Iraq, 2019. (photo Tallova/Dohnany)

Two sisters from Baghdad sing and play the ukulele in
the common area of Deir Maryam, Sulaymaniyah, Iraq.
(photo Tallova/Dohnany)

A young girl from Mosul, whose family fled the city,
learns piano in Deir Maryam, Sulaymaniyah, Iraq, 2019.
(photo Tallova/Dohnany)

The emblem of the monastery of Deir Maryam,
Sulaymaniyah, Iraq. (photo O'Neill)

Yazidi, Druze, Christian, and Muslim youth groups from Baghdad,
during a week-long peacebuilding workshop, celebrate a colleague's
birthday in Deir Maryam, Sulaymaniyah, Iraq, 2019.
(photo Cecchini)

A youth group from Baghdad enjoys some delicious
home cooking, during a workshop in Deir Maryam,
Sulaymaniyah, Iraq, 2019. (photo O'Neill)

Mass is celebrated by Fr. Jens and Fr. Jacques, as children rest on the floor in Deir Maryam, Sulaymaniyah, Iraq, 2019. (photo Cecchini)

Local children participate in Fr. Jens' mass in Deir Maryam, Sulaymaniyah, Iraq. (photo Cecchini)

A lone candle illuminates a portrait in memory of Fr. Paolo at the foot of the altar in the church of Deir Maryam, Sulaymaniyah, Iraq. (photo Cecchini)

Chapter 4: Harvest

Challenges

THERE WAS INITIAL MISTRUST regarding Fr. Paolo's IFD work that needed to be overcome, particularly when word got out about the Italian's close affinity with Islam. Practicing IFD in Mar Musa was not without teething difficulties as some locals felt patronized by the fact that foreigners—Fr. Paolo and most of his team—thought they could teach them something about religious coexistence with their neighbors. Christians were also incredulous that someone was reading the Qu'ran in a Catholic monastery. Cardinal-Bishop Daoud intervened and explicitly forbade this act but Fr. Paolo ignored him. Ironically, it might even have encouraged the recalcitrant Roman, for he delighted in upsetting those who were easily upset.

Many felt that it was condescending that these outsiders—particularly a loud Italian with his charm and swagger—could barge into their town and have something to offer, something to teach them, regarding coexistence between Muslims and Christians. "A foreigner arrives and thinks that he can do a lot and that it is easy to solve the problem with Islam and Christianity," says Fr Jens. "On one side, you have a local Christian population that have had a frustrating experience as their community dwindles over hundreds of years. Many Christians claim that they 'know' Islam, yet some are not even aware what Eid[1] is."[2] There was a constant push and pull between the cynics and the enthusiasts.

1. Eid al-Fitr is an important Muslim holy day that marks the end of Ramadan.

2. Petzold, Interview.

Years previously, a Lebanese priest, Fr. Abdo Badwi, was very critical of Fr. Paolo. "He [Fr. Paolo] is so in love with the idea of the Middle East and Islam that he doesn't fully take on board the experience of the local community," he said. "He is an Italian, not a local Christian, and he doesn't really know the historical or social backdrop to things and what we've had to put up with."[3]

The origins of some local people's initial hesitancy about IFD in Mar Musa arose from several factors. In some countries of the Middle East, it was crucial to assure participants that dialogue was not a front for a foreign political institution attempting to intervene in domestic affairs and intelligence gathering. There may have been an element of concern about the involvement of NGOs, foreign actors, or funders in Mar Musa at the onset, but the real doubts had deeper roots.

Some Christians liked the idea of the abandoned site being renovated—at least until they found out about Fr. Paolo's love of Islam. They were generally happy about efforts to rebuild the spot where Mar Musa stood. The monastery was in a terrible state of dilapidation and the priceless frescoes were in serious danger of being lost forever. However, when they realized how close Fr. Paolo was to Islam, they became much more suspicious.[4] Subsequently, they started to create more and more obstacles. In one striking incident, a week before Easter in 1992, the parish priest of Nebek, as well as other priests from the diocese, and a mob from the Christian community, arrived at the monastery in order to eject Fr. Paolo. It was violent and there was lots of screaming and high drama. It was quite the scene.[5]

Other elements in the Christian community did not like the idea of the monastery being renovated from the very onset. A restored monastery near their town did not suit the historical narrative of the besieged and dispossessed Christian minority. The symbolism of the ruins was more emblematic of their sense of injustice. "It is true that some Christians felt this way," says Fr. Jens.

3. Loosley, Interview.
4. Bashir, Interview.
5. Bashir, Interview.

"The Middle East is complicated and there are so many strands that are interconnected. Christians look back at past injustices and dispossession. Islam too, even today, is still preoccupied with the crusades. Both sides have deep wounds."[6]

Writer and poet Marius Kociejowski, who spent some time in Mar Musa in Fr. Paolo's company, concurs. Counterintuitively, Fr. Paolo was more trusted by Muslims than Christians, who believed the site of a ruined monastery "fed their [Christians] sense of marginalization (. . .) The only words against him [Fr. Paolo], I heard from Christians. Maybe some Muslims were distrustful at the beginning, but by and large he was incredibly popular with them."[7]

Fr. Paolo spoke in a blunt, caustic manner which not everyone appreciated. His direct vernacular—*terra terra* as they say in Italian—was both a help and a hindrance in convincing people of the Community's good intentions. "He was a bulldozer," Fr Jens states candidly. "He could get people really angry and start off on the wrong foot with them. That said, even if they were offended with him initially, he was still able to charm his way back in no time."[8]

These concerns about IFD and Mar Musa were eventually surmounted when it became clear that the real motives of the clergy were more than bona-fide. They were genuine in their efforts to bring the local community closer together—not divide them. Nor were there any doubts about the cross-religious dialogue they espoused being a front for evangelical efforts. Many organizations from Europe helped Mar Musa down through the years, and even though some people were suspicious initially, the locals would come to fully trust the Community.[9]

They overcame these issues by convincing people through the simple power of their words, actions, deeds. It was a critical moment in ensuring the ongoing success of the project across the Al-Khalil Community; a potential stumbling block had been

6. Petzold, Interview.
7. Kociejowski, Interview.
8. Petzold, Interview.
9. Bashir, Interview.

overcome.[10] It is important to note that the doubts and suspicions came not just from the lay community, but also, surprisingly, from the local religious hierarchy—the Christian churches.

The element of mistrust and confusion from some in the local community was exacerbated when several thought Fr. Paolo was not dealing with Christian members of the parish fairly. They thought he was treating Muslims more favorably and this led to jealousy and anger. Occasionally, Fr. Paolo may have indeed fanned the flames of discontent by being one-sided in his approach. His love of Islam blinkered him to his obvious subjectivity. Sometimes he would justify the unjustifiable for Islam because of his love for Muslims. He would make excuses for transgressions and provoke local Christians with his bias, angering and confusing them in the process.[11] The situation demanded tact and balance which the wilful Italian was often bereft of.

Some Christians were skeptical of authentic religious dialogue with Islam and whether discussion based on the shared theological practices and rituals between Christianity and Islam had any real meaning or relevance for them. This was a view sadly echoed by members of the religious hierarchy in Syria. During formal IFD in Mar Musa, there was always a focus on religious issues whenever possible. Some Christians remained hesitant, even going so far as saying that theologically it was impossible to undertake dialogue with Muslims.[12]

That said, it was not only Christians who were cautious of IFD efforts. Salah ad-Dīn Kuftaru, one of the foremost Muslim exponents of IFD in Syria, once infamously stated that he was against dialogue with Syrian Christians. It did not bode well that a member of the Syrian religious hierarchy involved in IFD had written cross-religious understanding off so casually.

Evidently there was doubt and a little cynicism, from both Christian and Muslim parties, about the relevance of this shared common space that Fr. Paolo and his team were attempting to forge.

10. Bashir, Interview.

11. Anonymous, Interview.

12. Bashir, Interview.

Some lay participants, from both sides of the religious landscape, were also troublesome and the specter of disagreement occasionally arose. Fr. Paolo, a practiced arbitrator like de Foucauld before him, would try to mediate in these situations. Sometimes there would be a troublesome guest or participant who would offend others and show a lack of respect. Christians criticizing Muslims or vice versa was counter-productive to the spirit of IFD. Occasionally people became argumentative, but Fr. Paolo always mediated these tricky situations expertly, diffusing the situation in the end. He would stress that they were not there to fight, and emphasized the mutual respect element.[13] This was a skill Fr Paolo would later use to good effect in the international arena, to plead, lobby, and negotiate for the democratic reform and freedom of Syria.

It is arguable that if Fr. Paolo had maintained more of a balanced focus, he would have been a more credible arbitrator for both religious sides. A source confirms that the monks and nuns tried to maintain a positive mood in IFD and discouraged those who sermonized imperiously. Everyone was welcome to dialogue as long as they did not impose or preach. Sometimes people were dogmatic.[14] However, Fr. Paolo who would offend people with his bluntness. For him confrontation was always preferable to evasion. Better to have things out in the open, even if that meant ruffling a few feathers in the process.

Having said that, no one sought total consensus during formal IFD. It was unfeasible and impractical considering the range of people who participated. Tolerating the intolerant was part of the process. A gentleman once chided them all at the end of a 10-day-long formal IFD conference for their perceived lack of agreement. "Once there was a person from the Goethe Institute that thought we had failed because there was no consensus after 10 days," says Fr. Jens. "But of course, there are some questions which are not always answerable."[15] As is to be expected when dealing with human beings, Mar Musa's IFD, in all its forms, was not without its

13. Bashir, Interview.
14. Anonymous, Interview.
15. Petzold, Interview.

short-term obstacles and limitations, but the long-term benefits would outweigh any perceived negatives.

The Syrian State and Mar Musa

There was no way that IFD efforts in Mar Musa would have been possible without cooperation with the government. Fr. Paolo had been criticized by some for being too close to Assad, but in reality all legitimate religious actors in Syria had to have a relationship with Damascus in order to achieve their goals. In this sense, Fr. Paolo was very much a pragmatist. Assad was indeed well aware of the presence of the Italian long before the shadow of unrest in March 2011. Every year Fr. Paolo had written a letter to Damascus urging the authorities to open up the country to reform, eventually culminating in the publication of his *Consensual Democracy* in 2011 which pleaded for a non-violent transition of power in the country.

In the Middle East, power, military might, and the political landscape, are all interwoven with religious belief. The government liked to keep a close eye on all religious actors in the Syrian arena to ensure it had sufficient influence and oversight. The state was co-opting IFD into its own form of interreligious dialogue as an inter-communal language in order to crush dissent.[16] It was a way of exploiting and controlling religious forces.

On the ground, it appears that the government supported only its own kind of formal religious dialogue and was suspicious of other modes of discourse. Government-sanctioned, institutionalized dialogue was always favored by Damascus as it quelled unruliness. Shady Hamadi, whose family fled Syria, stated that this was done in order to avoid strong inter- and intra-religious unity in the country. "The government were using the churches and imams in Syria to stay in power," says Hamadi. "In reality, the government was unofficially against *real* dialogue."[17] A country religiously united was not in their interests.

16. Szanto, "Inter-Religious Dialogue in Syria," 4.
17. Hamadi, Interview.

The government may have given Mar Musa permission to undertake formal IFD sessions, yet they did not overtly support or promote their efforts at dialogue.[18] This manifested itself in a blackout
on media attention for Mar Musa initiatives, as well as a dearth of
invitations for Mar Musa's monks and nuns to attend government-
run IFD sessions organized throughout the rest of Syria. The government were supporting and promoting only the kind of dialogue
they wanted. The would say things like, "we are equal," "we are all
together," and pay lip service to the idea of real IFD.[19]

There were other government-promoted IFD initiatives on
Syrian TV, but the Community received hardly any media exposure. The government would invite their own people to IFD
initiatives whom *they* would choose.[20] Damascus wanted full
control and IFD on their own terms, but what they were organizing was more of a charade. In the Arabic world, when you see
Christians and Muslims together on the TV, it is seen by many as
a political performance. Many of these IFD events are staged and
it changes nothing on the ground.[21] That said, in Mar Musa, the
annual seminars did also have an element of artifice, but the real
action was outside of the formal meetings, where relationships
were formed casually over breakfast or while doing the washing
up. That was the key difference.

The formal IFD undertaken in Mar Musa had always been observed by members of the state security services—the *Mukhabarat*.
Ba'athist tentacles were embroiled in most religious institutions
across Syria—that was a given. They actively monitored and ex-
erted [greater or lesser degrees of] control over all religious institutions. The government did not officially support IFD in Mar
Musa, and yet they were indirectly involved in the formal IFD
dialogue that took place there. Every official IFD session in Mar
Musa had a member of Assad's intelligence services present. Often
state-appointed religious figures were giving talks. The secret police

18. Bashir, Interview.
19. Bashir, Interview.
20. Bashir, Interview.
21. Bashir, Interview.

checked the various participants in attendance and sometimes even sat in on and took part in sessions. In Syria, their involvement in non-secular affairs was expected.[22] Yet the Community was granted a degree of autonomy—at the beginning at least.

However, even as early as 2009, Damascus' attitude to the initiatives of Mar Musa started to harden. The state began to clamp down as the monastery was seen as organizing a civil society with interest groups outside of their direct control. They thought that these workshops and the idea within them may have been dangerous in some way.[23] Some surmise this was due to a new Ba'athist policy on IFD projects generally, others say it was a change of personnel in the government during that period; but, either way, the interreligious experiment in Mar Musa suddenly started to be curtailed as the intelligence services' presence began to become more ubiquitous. They even began tapping their phones.[24]

Since the early 2000s, Fr. Paolo was sending letters to Damascus pleading for social and political reform. While it was uncommon for a prominent religious figure to be so conspicuously political, he had not been alone in Syrian civil society. There was the "Damascus Spring" of 2000, and the genuine political and social reform that was demanded at this time, via declarations signed by academics and artists across the country. With it came new hope for political progressiveness and a push back against the old order.

After the death of Hafez al-Assad in 2000, a buoyant optimism was evident across Syria. Soon after, the young western-educated ophthalmologist Bashar took power and promised economic overhaul. His older brother, Bassel, had been groomed for the presidency, but had tragically died in a car accident a few years earlier. There was a sudden growth spurt in civil society organizations that called for open dialogue and debate on Syria's future direction. Satirical political magazines that mocked the regime were even being published. However, the momentum was too quick and was eventually met with pushback against

22. Bashir, Interview.

23. Bashir, Interview.

24. Anonymous, Interview.

so-called politically liberal forces that were accused of threatening the country's stability. The crackdown of the "Damascus Winter" extinguished any hope that Bashar might be the liberalizing force many in Syrian society had wished for.

This was one of many political errors. Syrians were frustrated with the system, not necessarily the man in command. Anonymous sources confirm the short-sightedness of those who stood behind the levers of power at that time. In retrospect, the government had made a fatal miscalculation: criticism did not mean disloyalty. The popularity of the president—not the government—was immense. People were ridiculing how the system was functioning, not the president. The Ba'athists feared reform as they equated it with a loss of power, but, ironically, concessions would have seen them gain more control, more security. It was a fateful misstep.[25]

Fr. Paolo did cooperate with the government. Some criticized Fr. Paolo, saying he was a great friend of Assad, but this seems unfair. "Of course he needed to work with the government. It was impossible not to," says friend and confidante, Shady Hamadi. "He was given some free reign to work with interreligious dialogue in Mar Musa, but alone—and without the support of anyone."[26] Fr. Paolo cooperated with the state as long as he could have relative religious freedom to organize his IFD sessions in Mar Musa and continue with his hospitality work. There was a caveat: for this autonomy and a loosening of the shackles of strict regime control over religious life, came the implicit notion of loyalty to Damascus. This was a dangerous arrangement, considering the outspoken nature of the man in charge at Mar Musa. Compliance was not in the Italian's blood.

State surveillance of IFD in Mar Musa obviously had an influence on how the participants felt during seminars, and also on the topics open for discussion. It undoubtedly oriented group dialogue towards inoffensive theological themes as opposed to those of a more social or political bent. It meant IFD sessions were rather

25. Anonymous, Interview.
26. Hamadi, Interview.

apolitical in nature and skirted around sensitive topics associated with the government and Assad, unless they had a social context—but even then they were limited.[27] This explains the tendency to veer away from more risky secular dialogue to the safer confines of theological, cognitive discussion.

Syria had been under martial law for almost half a century, and people had become accustomed to living in a country where surveillance and monitoring, of even the most innocuous activity, was commonplace. Surprisingly, this did not decrease attendance in IFD sessions. "They [the *Mukhabarat*] were always there. People knew who they were and why they were there,"[28] states one anonymous source.

For any outsider, this might seem like an oppressive environment in which to undertake and participate in IFD; on the contrary, for many Syrians, it was simply the norm. Subsequently, there was an implicit shared awareness, among organizers and participants alike, about what could and could not be talked about during IFD sessions. It was not the Community's main aim to venture too far into the political arena for obvious reasons—mostly they would avoid that. The main focus was on faith and the relationship between different religions[29] It remains to be seen whether this focus was due to the security services presence or not. Nevertheless, there was undeniably an element of subterfuge. The involvement of intelligence agencies necessitated it.

One detractor of IFD criticizes the facade of organized formal IFD, seeing it as a shallow PR veneer to showcase the more substantial work of openness and hospitality espoused by Al-Khalil through their more effective informal dialogue efforts. There were often five people from the secret service present at formal seminars. The Community wanted to do something but they also had to be careful. Discussions that branched out into different directions did of course happen, but the informal dialogue of daily life was the one that probably engaged people more. The principles

27. Bashir, Interview.

28. Anonymous, Interview.

29. Bashir, Interview.

elaborated on in the formal sessions then crystallized into how to receive different people, day to day, through the hospitality work.[30]

The Catholic Church and Mar Musa

Rather than supporting and encouraging IFD efforts, church leaders viewed the activity in Mar Musa with suspicion. Despite aligning with the ideals of *Nostra Aetate*, the work of Fr. Paolo and his team was met with some intransigence and doubt from other Catholic and Christian churches around Syria. They were unwilling to fully get behind the decree and support the broader Community of Al-Khalil in their interreligious work. While there were pockets of support for Fr. Paolo's dialogue, sadly many of the hierarchy remained at best unconvinced, at worst highly skeptical—a reaction that unashamedly flew in the face of the principles of 1965's *Nostra Aetate* from the Vatican II Council which urged cooperation, tolerance, and a demystification of the religious *other*.

Many Christian churches and people in the East have a cultural, historical, and emotional difficulty with Islam. This adversarial attitude seems best exemplified by Cardinal-Bishop Daoud (formerly Archbishop of Homs). He found the theology of Fr. Paolo and his promotion of Mar Musa's unique form of interreligious practices questionable. For Cardinal-Bishop Daoud, this tarnished the Italian's attempts at interreligious cooperation among the religious communities of the area. He had misgivings about its real motives as he did not like the uncompromising way Fr. Paolo presented his relationship with Islam.[31]

This culminated in Patriach Daoud's official questioning of an article written by Fr. Paolo called "In Praise of Syncretism." He sent this to Rome for examination along with Mar Musa's monastic constitution, to ensure there were no heretical practices being undertaken. This was done via the Congregation for the Doctrine of the Faith—a body of various religious and lay figures, originally

30. Anonymous, Interview.

31. Bashir, Interview.

founded in 1542 to defend points of Christian tradition which might be threatened due to new and unacceptable doctrines. This overseeing committee enforced proper traditional religious practices that were fully in line with the church's teachings. However, much to Patriach Daoud's chagrin, the verdict returned over a year later more complementary than critical. Rome had found nothing problematic whatsoever in the theological teachings of Fr. Paolo and the monastic constitution of Mar Musa. Both received the decree of *Nulla Ostra* (nothing forbidden) from Pope Benedict XVI in 2006.[32] The highest Catholic authority was publically vindicating Al-Khalil and Mar Musa. The Catholic Church in Syria remained more dubious about IFD in Mar Musa than the Vatican.[33] The religious Community were pleasantly surprised, thinking they would have had more problems theologically regarding their strong stance on dialogue with Islam—but that turned out not to be the case.

For Fr Paolo, Rome's decision reaffirmed his unapologetic passion for Islam. A life-long philosophy he had nurtured for years had been endorsed by his peers. Something the Syriac Catholic Church had viewed as bordering on radical, i.e., loving Islam, blending some religious practices, and unapologetically encouraging dialogue between Christians and Muslims, was actually rather standard after all. Despite the Roman *Nulla Ostra*, Cardinal-Bishop Daoud, and other members of the Catholic hierarchy in Syria, were displeased with such an interpretation. Christians in the East consider this a very delicate theological issue which should take into account the historical element of the region. The church officially teaches *inclusiveness* but often this is ignored if it does not suit your agenda.[34] The older, more conservative religious leaders, felt that the European clergy who had come to Syria had not really experienced war and turmoil like they had. The Community's European roots had negated whatever good they had intended—at least in the minds of those native religious leaders.

32. Bashir, Interview.

33. Bashir, Interview.

34. Bashir, Interview.

The Vatican's progressive ecumenism had its limitations however. Some Orthodox priests wanted to become monks in Mar Musa. Formally priests should become Catholic when they enter the monastery, but the Community really wanted to permit them to remain Orthodox. They asked if an Orthodox deacon could become a monk in Mar Musa and be ordained a priest, but Rome refused to sanction such a move.[35] Needless to say, it is crucial to examine the roots of the issue that the Catholic hierarchy had with Mar Musa's perceived radicalism.

Religious *Harmonization*: Between Inculturation and Syncretism

The term, Church of Islam, is a common theme in Fr. Paolo's writings. In ecclesiastical circles at least, it was deemed inflammatory, consequently, he was subject to criticism for using it. For the Italian, a Church of Islam was a compromise between both religions—a form of inculturation.[36] Inculturation is mentioned numerous times in his book *Innamorato dell'Islam, Credente in Gesù [Lover of Islam. Believer in Jesus]*. It is a recognized term and common in ecumenical theology, but it was Fr. Paolo's reappraisal of it that might have caused consternation with those of a more conservative bent.

According to Dennis Doyle, author and academic at the University of Dayton, "The Concept of Inculturation in Roman Catholicism is a theological consideration. Inculturation is the term that Catholic leaders and theologians have used in recent decades to denote a process of engagement between the Christian Gospel and a particular culture."[37] It is a form of religious and cultural exchange that benefits both sides mutually, a means of incorporating the gospel into a specific foreign culture. You use the words of the scripture to engage with a different, religiously *other,* way of life.

35. Bashir, Interview.
36. Dall'Oglio, *Innamorato dell'Islam*, 43.
37. Doyle, "The Concept of Inculturation," 1.

That said, the concept behind a Church of Islam points to a more subversive interpretation of mere inculturation.

Fr Paolo was not the first to coin the term Church of Islam. The last Patriach of the Melkite Church used a similar expression—a Church of Islam/Arabs. Like Fr Paolo's concept, it was related to the incorporation of the Christian faith into a Muslim context. A church of Islamic culture. The church and the Islamic world are side by side but some of the local churches did not want to be associated with Arabs. They preferred to be distinct and separate.[38]

Local churches did not want a blending together of various faiths for fears of diluting their identity. They were closed to this cross-religious experience, whereas Fr. Paolo fervently embraced it. Since the beginning of Islam, churches were more insular in order to protect their ideas, to preserve their power, but Fr. Paolo was always open, fluid, malleable. Qualities that could be troublesome for a section of the religious order. Fr. Paolo was unusual as he simply did not fit into any category or mold. He disliked people who were dogmatic and spoke in absolutes. He was open to all ideas, even syncretism—the blending together of cross-religious practices.[39] For him, the world was syncretic by its very nature, and while never fully embracing the religiously provocative concept of syncretism, he had more than a fleeting dalliance with the notion.

Fr. Jens, now at the helm in Deir Maryam, Sulaymaniyah, talks about Fr. Paolo's usage of the term inculturation. A standard definition is an interpretation of the gospel through the prism of a different culture, yet this could be problematic as inculturation is a Western-derived term from the Roman Catholic European Church and has particular connotations. Perhaps the Eastern Church needed a new phrase that better suited its historical and cultural backdrop. "We do not come from a foreign church—our members are Eastern and we are part of the Syriac Catholic Church—so we are not outsiders," says Fr. Jens. "Fr. Paolo became more Arab than the Arabs in some ways. As clergy of the Syriac Catholic Church,

38. Bashir, Interview.
39. Bashir, Interview.

73

everything we do has a historical context and our rituals are a remembrance of these historical imprints."[40]

Fr. Jens agrees that Fr. Paolo's talk of a Church of Islam was viewed as rather rabble rousing in church circles. Some of the hierarchy were open to the idea of interreligious education but, unlike Fr. Paolo, they did not see the inherent good in Islam. Fr. Paolo's use of the word inculturation, meant that religion had to translate its essence into this new foreign culture. "Personally, what I think Fr. Paolo was attempting was something called incarnation and not inculturation," states Fr. Jens. "Christianity can be placed within an Arab context and still be Christian."[41]

When I visited Deir Maryam in Iraq, as in Mar Musa, everyone took their shoes off before entering the church. According to Fr. Jens, this is not a form of inculturation per se, since it is intrinsic to the culture of the local church there. He explains that in Mar Musa it was done for three reasons: they wanted to be close to Islam and create a sacral space that was appealing to local Muslims; the old churches had a long history of doing this in places like Maaloula;[42] they were working with goats and it made sense—practically speaking.[43] Religious harmonization is a term that can encompass Fr. Paolo's and Fr Jens' concepts of inculturation and incarnation respectively.

While Rome had given Fr. Paolo the green light on his specific theology, in Syria some remained unconvinced at the practices being carried out in Mar Musa. Fr. Paolo decided to say mass in Arabic—rather uncommon for Syrian monasticism which would normally have used Syriac—the specific Aramaic dialect used by Syrian-rite Christians. The Syrian Catholic Church normally uses a mixture of Syriac and Arabic.

40. Petzold, Interview.

41. Petzold, Interview.

42. One of the oldest surviving monasteries in Syria is St. Sarkis Eastern Catholic Monastic Complex in Maaloula. Built on the site of a pagan temple, Maaloula was the scene of several fierce battles between rebel forces and the government during the Syrian Civil War.

43. Petzold, Interview.

Other examples of religious harmonization or synthesis with the specific host culture included not only leaving shoes outside the chapel before entering, but also sitting and kneeling on carpets—similar to those in mosques (there were no pews); the way they placed bibles on stands exactly like those used in mosques to hold the Qur'an, or their use of specific Islamic vocabulary to describe Mar Musa's frescoes or the rich history of the monastery.[44] The monastic tradition of praying while facing east, toward the rising sun, head bowed, must have also left an impression on visiting Muslim pilgrims in Mar Musa.

Fr. Paolo employed prostration for prayer—body outstretched, hands forward and touching the ground. It is also the sign of abject submission to the will of God during ordination and comes from an older tradition, but outwardly, at least, this was reminiscent of Muslim worshippers. Again it might be easy to misinterpret such an act from a Catholic monk, and the impact such behavior may have had on visiting pilgrims. "Christians might be rather confused as they may not be aware of that older tradition," explains Fr. Jens. "Fr. Paolo tried to consider and show respect to *all* the traditions of the church, but the act is not as ambiguous as you might think."[45]

For Fr. Paolo, these small concessions were the "discarded seed that allows the whole dough to rise for the food of many."[46] These seemingly inconsequential gestures held great significance for the solidarity they betokened with the local Muslim community. As noted earlier, Fr. Paolo and other members of the religious Community observed Ramadan each year, out of respect for the Muslim staff of the monastery. He considered it another form of Lent, urging fellow Christians to join him in solidarity with their neighbors by fasting during this time.

Such camaraderie is highlighted in Yasmin Fedda's 2012 movie, *A Tale of Two Syrias*. The narrator describes an explicit act of unity from the clergy of Mar Musa where they are shown

44. Bashir, Interview.
45. Petzold, Interview
46. Dall'Oglio, *Innamorato dell'Islam*, 62.

carrying out an animal sacrifice on an Islamic holy day. It was a physical manifestation of their belief and respect for dialogue. They joined in with celebrations for Eid—the holy festival that signals the end of Ramadan.

In the telling scene of the movie, a live goat is carried down the steps to the low wall by two helpers in Mar Musa. Fr. Paolo is heard saying, "We ask God to accept this offering. We want to show our love and cooperation; to express our love for God, Muslims, and all the people in this part of the world. The people who lived in this valley were shepherds. They lived off this blessing here [points to the doomed goat]. So we ask God to protect us all."[47] Fr. Paolo then proceeds to slit the beast's throat as quickly as possible as it gasps its last breaths. The hand that had just held the poor creature's throat, as it gushed warm jets of dark blood, is then used to make a visible crimson handprint on the wall of the monastery. He concludes with the words, *"al-ḥamdu lillāh"* [thanks be to God].

Even the language used in the Community of Al-Khalil was specific. In Syria, Muslims would say *al-ḥamdu lillāh*—for thanks be to God, however, Christians would say *shukr-lillāh*. Fr. Paolo and Fr. Jens both used the Islamic way—they spoke Islamically. They did not speak in typical Christian form. Some surmise that they could do this because they were not local and not held up to typical tribal standards.[48]

During my visit to Deir Maryam in Sulaymaniyah, I observed some interesting practices in the church there. Everywhere there were echoes of Mar Musa: some of the congregation sat on the floor on rugs, in a circle, with shoes removed. The Eucharist was administered without pressing questions as to whether one was baptized or not. Some of the younger children felt comfortable enough to doze on the thick carpet under them, in the warm, convivial surrounds of Fr Jens' mass.

The spirit of cross-cultural appreciation that is characteristic of Fr. Paolo's Church of Islam, has developed further and lives on in other Al-Khalil communities. Fr. Jens' congregation also

47. Fedda, *A Tale of Two Syrias*, 23:00–24:30.
48. Szanto, Interview.

consisted of members of the Filipino and Indian community. He made small concessions to adapt the mass to their culture, to make them feel more at home, more welcome. "Fr. Jens adopted some of their songs," explains Prof. Szanto. "For Christmas, he went to the Faruk Medical Hospital in order to celebrate with them because that's where most Filipinos and Indians worked."[49] I discovered that the mass was changed a little for them too. Some hymns were in Hindi. They also had the opportunity to prepare projects together for specific religious festivals and celebrations. In this way, inculturation could be seen as reflecting not just the culture where they were based, but also that of their congregation.

Some churches in the Middle East have become like those in the West, without taking into account the culture of their surroundings. In Mar Musa's chapel, everyone gathered in a circle on the floor, very much like a Sufi *Halafa*. Middle East culture has become synonymous with Islam and some churches there have become inculturated to the West; but there's nothing Islamic about taking off your shoes. Interestingly, some Christians don't do that anymore, which Marshall Hodgson—Islamic studies academic, author, and historian—refers to as *Islamicate*. Fr. Paolo was romantic in the way he tried to inculturate. He consciously took deliberate forms or practices from *Islamicate* culture, which have become synonymous with Islam and that are no longer perceived as Christian.[50] Al-Khalil and Mar Musa railed against this watering down of Eastern culture and unapologetically embraced the living Islamic world around them.

Fr. Paolo refused to accept that there was anything unusual about the practices being carried out across Al-Khalil. He defined what they were doing as so-called radical inculturation. In his article "In Praise of Syncretism," he boldly states:

> "Here by radical we mean something that goes beyond folklore, clothing, carpets on the floor, bare feet in church and the fluent use of Muslim religious language (. . .) Here we are trying to be a seed tossed, that permits

49. Szanto, Interview.
50. Szanto, Interview.

the earth to give fruit (. . .) Here we are trying to wed Islam to Jesus of Nazareth living in the Church."[51]

Beyond inculturation, even radical inculturation, the term syncretism also suggests religious inclusivity, though it goes somewhat further. It involves the blending of distinct theological beliefs into something altogether new. Some consider it a negation of authentic dialogue, as it conjoins a plethora of elements from different religions into some kind of a new whole. There is criticism that this religious cross-pollination is confusing and disregards the virtue of the religions involved. For Fr Paolo, syncretism's blending of multiple practices did not water down the essence of religion, instead, it facilitated true exchange of interreligious thought as multiple syncretic elements could coexist side by side, in harmony.

Such was his affinity with Muslims, Fr. Paolo had no qualms about undertaking measures that approached the concept of syncretism tentatively while never fully embracing it. He was a realist. The pull and push of the syncretic influence on cultural and religious life was evident in its reciprocity, openly admitting, "human culture is syncretic in nature. Religious belief, an essential dimension of cultural life, is radically, clearly syncretic."[52] It was inescapable. He had an intuitive awareness that many—Christians and non-Christians alike—were uncomfortable with syncretism because of the fear of its potential erosion of identity and power.[53] Pillars of control for the establishment.

The objections raised by opponents of syncretism include the allegations that syncretism is relativist, a religious compromise, and that not all religious rituals are appropriate for an IFD setting. This was particularly true in terms of communal interreligious prayer. Many of the people I interviewed, advocated the safe ground of shared silences. This was happening in Mar Musa, as were recitations of the LORD's Prayer and Muslim participation in the Prayers of the Faithful. However, it is Fr. Paolo's harnessing of the mystical

51. Dall'Oglio, "In Praise of Syncretism," paragraph 22.

52. Dall'Oglio, *Innamorato dell'Islam*, 55.

53. Dall'Oglio, *Innamorato dell'Islam*, 54.

and spiritual elements of Sufism as a link between Christianity and Islam that is most remarkable, and represents a tentative manifestation of syncretism in a Mar Musa context.

Analysis of Christian and Muslim scripture and texts by both lay and religious participants, and the trance-like chanting that they performed, joined all those present in its shared embrace. Fr. Paolo had spent some time with the Sufi milieu in Damascus during his formative years. Social contact with them had rubbed off since he was actively harnessing the meditative and spiritual aspect of Sufism and its close affinity with music. It formed the ideal inclusive neutral ground that both Christians and Muslims could connect through, bridging differences, thereby forging a radical new space, transcending the narrower confines of both Christian and Muslim doctrine.

Fr. Jens agrees that syncretism is everywhere. There are so many elements in mass where other religions play a part. It is inescapable. Regarding the Sufi chanting and the *Zkir* that Fr. Paolo so loved, there is the renowned old monkish chanting from France that can last for hours and be quite hypnotic. The Sufis do not have a monopoly on this, but what they do is succinctly express this beauty and get in touch with its essence. Fr. Paolo was equally fascinated by Zen Buddhism and Japanese flute music. "Fr. Paolo's main focus was Islam and he did alienate Christians because of this overt love," according to Fr. Jens, "but right and left of that, he found other avenues that were flourishing and intriguing. Inculturation is a sensitive concept as you come from another culture, and you need to be careful not to come at it from a position of superiority."[54] It needed a delicate touch.

Fr. Jens is also eager to point out that even though this inclination toward Sufism may outwardly seem syncretic, in practice, it sprang from more practical grounds; sitting on the floor of the church is like a Sufi *Halafa*, however, churches in the Middle East did not have pews in the past so this was practical. "It is not strictly syncretism as through these actions we are remembering the past

54. Petzold, Interview.

and the culture of the East," Fr. Jens explains. "People at home, and in sacred spaces always left their shoes outside." [55]

Fr. Paolo's unadulterated love of Sufi chanting referenced Islamic culture. He tried to translate Christianity not just into an Arab context, but into an Islamic one.[56] It was neither inculturation nor syncretism, but a form of religious harmonization that was unique to Mar Musa and the Community.

Prof. Bongiovanni talked about Fr. Paolo's rather non-conventional theological practices in Mar Musa and Rome's views on his Interfaith Dialogue sessions which began a quarter of a century after *Nostra Aetate*. He states:

> "Perhaps the experience of Paolo took time to be understood by the church and the Vatican outside of the immediate context. I think at the beginning it was difficult. Yes, dialogue is important, but how do you go about this? All experiences of religious dialogue need to be discerned or understood."[57]

Yes, Paolo was viewed as a maverick within church circles. His outspoken and mischievous nature meant that he might even have taken a wicked pleasure in the consternation he aroused among the entrenched and inflexible conservatism of some of the establishment. Nevertheless, he was acutely aware how his cross-blending of practices might be perceived, not only by the religious hierarchy, but also by followers of Islam. He had to carefully navigate the space that demarcated the spiritual overlap between both Islam and Christianity. If he pushed things too far, he could potentially lose his legitimacy as an arbitrator for both sides.

It was not just the Catholic establishment who viewed the blending of cross-religious practices with concern. Fr. Paolo was one of those responsible for organizing Pope John Paul II's historic visit to Umayyad Mosque in Damascus in 2001—the first time a pontiff had visited a holy site of Islam. During the organization of the event,

55. Petzold, Interview.
56. Szanto, Interview.
57. Bongiovanni, Interview.

which Fr. Paolo had closely worked on, a problem arose when a bishop suggested that there should be a common prayer during the mass—a shared Islamic-Christian prayer. Fr. Paolo agreed—how wonderful it would be that this magnificent mosque could become a shared space of worship for one day.

The Saudis and some others immediately started remonstrating that letting unbelievers pray there would be an act of heresy in the mosque. Prayer for them was seen as synonymous with Christian mass and this was totally unacceptable. As a result, sadly, no common prayer was allowed. Instead the Pope prayed in silence in front of the shrine of St. John the Baptist. He gave a speech outside the mosque in the marble courtyard.[58]

What was happening in Mar Musa existed in a space outside of terms such as religious inculturation and syncretism. Fr. Paolo's harmonization of the disparate threads of both creeds was unique. He had always wanted to follow in Jesus' footsteps, and, like Jesus, he was lured toward the more subversive approach. Yet to say he was a revolutionary or a rebel is lazy and simplistic, for he was fiercely traditional in many respects. He championed a shared form of theology—encompassing both Christian and Muslim ideals—that could act as a counterweight to the widening schism between both camps.

Mar Musa and the larger Community of Al-Khalil represented a synthesis of Christianity and Islam; they were moving steadily closer to Fr. Paolo's concept of a Church of Islam. The heart of the Community transcended the rigid limitations and negative connotations of syncretism and was less culturally superior than Western-defined inculturation. Al-Khalil was not explicitly syncretic, but like bees, anything that they regarded as good, they borrowed from it.[59] In essence, they were synthesizing their sense of this double belonging to both Christianity and Islam.

Even though Fr. Paolo's rather controversial harmonizing of cross-religious practices sadly alienated some elements of the church, he was partially successful in realizing his ambitious

58. Bashir, Interview.
59. Bashir, Interview.

theological concept of a Church of Islam. It is regrettable that the other Christian churches throughout Syria did not view Fr. Paolo's particular brand of religious harmonization more favorably. If there had been less inflexibility from Fr. Paolo, more subtlety, with an eye toward bringing the more conservative elements of the Christian hierarchy onboard, perhaps the inclusive message at the core of their IFD work could have been disseminated better.

If Fr. Paolo had been more compromising, less vehement in his unapologetic mixing and matching of customs and rituals, which occasionally bordered on the irreverent—even heretical, to those of a more conservative persuasion—he may have won more adherents across the wider religious community in Syria. Instead, many remained on the sidelines, suspicious and distrustful.

With a different approach, tactics, Fr. Paolo could have been a conduit for the wider popularization of his message. Subsequently, the Community of Mar Musa and beyond may have been able to break free of their church- and state-imposed isolation regarding IFD, thereby propelling their inclusivist and progressive message of religious harmonization and pluralism to a much wider spectrum of society.

The Movement of a Butterfly's Wings: The Social Ripple of IFD

The hospitality-focused IFD of Mar Musa and the wider Community constituted an ongoing experience that complemented—and in many respects overshadowed—the formal yearly seminars. It was the shared religious space they offered up that was the truly unique phenomenon. Unfortunately, the results of interreligious dialogue can be difficult to measure. Yet, there is evidence that the Community's sustained efforts certainly reaped a social reward in the villages in the monastery's vicinity.

Formal IFD in Mar Musa was existing in a government-imposed vacuum, contained, and unable to achieve its full potential. There was little opportunity to synchronize these efforts with other centers, in order to push their message of interreligious tolerance and advocacy of a civil society to the distant corners of the country. That said, the shared informal dialogue the religious clergy in Mar Musa championed—stressing unconditional friendship and hospitality—was the most effective counterweight to violence, malevolence, and political and social manipulation of religious difference. The message at the heart of the Al-Khalil Community aspired to a time when there would be no more ignorance or fear of the religious *other*.

Prof. Loosley thinks this dialogue of everyday life certainly outshone the more rigid and formal meetings in its sustained and ongoing focus. "The general friendships and daily interactions had more effect than the seminars. They were a life-long thing,"[60] she states. The friendship, gestures, and routine of daily life in the monastery was where the core of the Community's message coalesced and strengthened.

Al-Khalil's formal and informal IFD projects actively involved the poor, lay people, women, the youth, the disenfranchised, and voiceless in society. By empowering the powerless, they implicitly advocated that power in society be more evenly distributed—a radical enough concept in Assad's Syria. "We were speaking about theology at the formal meetings and conferences. However, they were not Mar Musa. Mar Musa was the other work we did," Fr Jens confirms. "The seminars had minimal impact—let's be honest."[61] The informal dialogue—the dialogue of daily life—was the one that probably engaged people more. It transpires that the formal dialogue was only a means to an end. It was a way to form, promote, and showcase the Community by publicizing what they really wanted to do—hospitality.[62]

Yes, the largely government-sanctioned formal IFD events tried to involve grassroots work that incorporated all segments of local society. Whenever possible operating outside of any direct organizational control of Damascus, the monks and nuns had some autonomy over IFD seminar structure, topics for

60. Loosley, Interview.
61. Petzold, Interview.
62. Petzold, Interview.

discussion, participant selection, etc. However, it was sporadic, limited in scope and contained, while the dialogue of daily life was ongoing, and an authentic process *in progress*. It was not a publicity stunt nor was it staged. It was a real and genuine process of discovery which gave birth to strong friendships. People still have great relationships with each other in these areas.[63] Powerful cross-tribal bonds had been bolstered, standing resolute in the face of growing sectarian instability.

The long-term result of this religious intermingling, through both informal and formal IFD efforts in Mar Musa, was striking— both at a personal and social level. The atmosphere that permeated Mar Musa helped people who had always grappled with issues of identity. "I was looking for a way to explain to myself what I was. Who I was," states Shady Hamadi. "Mar Musa was a way to describe and approach my own religion as a Muslim. Then, I understood that I couldn't be a Muslim without thinking of myself as a Christian too. In fact, I am a very much a Muslim man who also considers himself a Christian."[64]

Hamadi's epiphany was not a direct result of formal IFD efforts, but was brought about by the space offered in Mar Musa. It was inclusive, reflective, and there was no judgment. For many, Mar Musa made sense; it offered a safe common area, free from the strict doctrine of either faith. It was a reimagining of the traditional monastery, as clergy and laity had little to no hierarchical distinction, with non-denominational spiritualism elevated above inflexible religious dogma.

Mar Musa's social impact on the communities around the monastery should not be downplayed. For Fr. Paolo, language was key to unlocking the treasure trove of true Interfaith Dialogue. "When he was in the church speaking Arabic it seemed so natural," says Hamadi. "The possibility for dialogue with Christian Arabs and Muslim Arabs is so obvious—they share the same expressions, language etc. Dialogue is natural."[65]

63. Bashir, Interview.
64. Hamadi, Interview.
65. Hamadi, Interview.

Visits from the monks and nuns outside Mar Musa to the local communities were common—including between prominent religious figures. There was a closeness between the monastery and local Sufis and imams. The monks would regularly visit mosques in the village.[66] This was important as it sent a powerful signal to parishioners regarding their religious leaders' validation of IFD efforts. It was mature moral leadership in action. When religious authority figures openly engaged and discussed, that implicit message of tolerance was transmitted down to their respective flocks. It was a strikingly emphatic message of coexistence. Naturally, this had a positive knock-on effect between parishioners. Close friendships lasting years were formed during this time. The monks and nuns visited local Muslim communities and stayed in touch with the pilgrims who had visited Mar Musa.[67]

The Community were aware of the power of dialogue to affect change and the slow-release synergy of its inclusive message. Consequently, they excelled at molding Mar Musa's space into somewhere people could come together and engage with each other in a neutral, welcoming zone—free from prejudice. A place where, paradoxically, through exposure to other faiths, you could gain a deeper understanding of your own.

Fr. Paolo was convinced we could overcome our common differences. Religious coexistence was not some lofty, abstract ideal, to aspire to in the distant future; on the contrary, it was real and achievable, despite the obstacles. In an interview, Fr. Paolo once summarized his ambitious plans for his little interreligious monastery near Nebek. He said he wanted it to be "a point of spiritual attraction in the country" and one with an "international ethos."[68] He was successful. The monastery's name remains on everyone's lips. Few visitors to Syria can say they have not heard of Mar Musa.

The Interfaith Dialogue that was championed throughout the entire monastic Community of Al-Khalil in Syria and Iraq were rare beacons on the IFD religious landscape of the region. The IFD they

66. Bashir, Interview.
67. Bashir, Interview.
68. COSV, "Deir Mar Musa Documentary," 05:00–10:00.

advocated, encompassed, to varying degrees, many different forms of dialogue. It was formal and informal, spontaneous and planned, ceremonial and every-day, grand and mundane.

Undoubtedly, politics remains an obstacle to true interfaith peace work as total autonomy and control are never fully possible. Dialogue is more fruitful when it is uninhibited. Nevertheless, against these odds, the monks and nuns still successfully harnessed the limited means at their disposal, and, under more than challenging conditions, created something exceptional, tirelessly chipping away at the monolithic stumbling blocks of conflict, barbarism, mistrust, hate, fear. A bulwark against those in power who sow suspicion to divide people.

The practicalities of pushing out the core of Al-Khalil's IFD philosophy across Syria were unrealistic. "It was successful in an underground sense. To do it large scale you need a lot of people," says Fr. Jens. "It was exhausting and it was done the only way it was possible at the time with the means at our disposal." [69] Yes, they could have done things better in the Community, but they simply did not have the experience, man-power nor knowledge back then. Mar Musa was a small place. Subsequently, the effect was limited.[70]

As things stood, various elements within Syrian Christian churches also felt alienated by Fr. Paolo. The hierarchy's conservativism, intransigence, and ingrained historical suspicion of the *other*, meant that Fr. Paolo's *Nostra Aetate*-inspired efforts at interreligious friendship-building, never got the full weight of their institutional power behind. Ironically, in the minds of some, the feisty Italian had inadvertently become the very epitome of the *other* that he had fought so hard to demystify. Instead of flourishing, their formal IFD floundered within its own self-contained microcosm of Syrian society.

Even though never promoted at a nation-wide level, it is clearly evident that the IFD of Mar Musa had a positive impact on inter-religious local relationships. The town of Nebek is still very

69. Petzold, Interview.

70. Petzold, Interview.

proud of the good-neighborliness of its inhabitants. The houses that were reconstructed during the war by Christians and Muslims are a source of great joy for locals and clergy alike. To see Christian and Muslim children growing up *together* brings hope. The Community remain optimistic that all their projects—past and present—may help make a small step toward future peace and coexistence.

Fr. Paolo and his team celebrated breaking down barriers of ignorance, and the open, joyful appreciation of those things which we all share: friendship, mutual understanding, help in times of need, camaraderie. Respect and empathy were the bedrock of their work. It was their raison d'être.

Politicization: Implications

Fr. Paolo's delicate balancing act of negotiation and compromise with the powers in Damascus, in addition to Mar Musa's rather fractious relationship with other Christian churches in Syria, would again be brought into the spotlight as unrest swept through the country in early 2011. The scourge of underlying sectarianism would slowly take hold as the fragile secular veneer of Syrian society began to disintegrate.

When the interreligious bricolage started splintering, Fr. Paolo's increasing political activism and loud criticism of the regime made him something of a figurehead for the opposition. People rallied to support him during Abuna Paolo Day on December 4, 2011, when protestors dedicated one of the usual anti-government Friday protests to him.[71] They wanted to emphasize how religion could unite, not divide; the politically outspoken Italian embodied this. By now Fr. Paolo was being increasingly seen as a religious pariah and nuisance for both the church and state. He would soon be asked to leave the country over fears for his safety.

In true Christian fashion, the central pillar of Mar Musa's ideology was hospitality. *Whoever* came to the monastery should

---

71. Falciatore, "Who is Father Dall'Oglio," line 38–40.

find an open door, food, accommodation, a space. They would not be judged but instead could find understanding, acceptance, shelter, a safe haven. Shady Hamadi, whose father was a victim of regime torture, says that this took on added significance when opposition members sought sanctuary in Mar Musa after their release. The Community welcomed victims of government torture. "Mar Musa was a refuge for people because you couldn't talk about what happened to in prison after you left," Hamadi states. "There they could get some support, psychological assistance, to help them overcome the trauma. Fr. Paolo was welcoming them as his children. He knew what was going on."[72]

The Community gave shelter to political dissidents and victims of torture—without hesitation. To refuse was unconscionable. They thereby became tarnished with the brush of political partisanship. For Fr. Paolo and his team, Mar Musa's welcome had to be inclusive and egalitarian *without* exception.

The ramifications of Mar Musa's unquestioning acceptance of those who were being persecuted by the state were far-reaching. There would be consequences for a Catholic Community unconditionally offering refuge to ex-political prisoners. In Assad's eyes, those seeking refuge were enemies of the state. Yet, the monks and nuns of Mar Musa saw those fleeing terror in human terms: fathers, husbands, brothers, sons—people who had been mistreated. They were accepted into the Community without judgment. This was the monks' and nuns' religious obligation, nevertheless, that compassionate gesture would still be seen as a profoundly seditious political act.

Syrian filmmaker and opposition activist, Bassel Shehadeh, was killed in Homs in May 2012. Friends and family of the deceased struggled to find a place of sanctuary to mourn the passing of their loved one in safety. Mar Musa's hand of welcome was outstretched when others were notably withdrawn. As the political situation intensified, other Christian churches took a collective step back, to avoid being seen as allied with any one side. Shehadeh's friends went to Mar Musa for refuge and Fr. Paolo opened the

72. Hamadi, Interview.

monastery's door for them. They had wanted to arrange a prayer service for him in Damascus but they were refused permission by the authorities and some people were arrested. For many this was a typical example of how the churches were connected to the Syrian government and controlled by them.[73]

Fr. Paolo was a prominent religious figure during the early days of unrest. He fearlessly spoke out against government torture, railed at the murder of innocent protesting civilians on Syrian streets, and was a champion of peaceful resistance and social justice. During this time, the overwhelming silence of the church, including the Vatican, amid the ongoing brutality of the crackdowns was deafening for him. This was not the time to equivocate when people were being murdered. He remained a vocal defender of the Syrian people in their quest for democratic, social, and economic reform—irrespective of their religious affiliation. They were *his* people. He had to speak and speak he did. Silence was complicity.

73. Hamadi, Interview.

Chapter 5: **Brotherhood and Solidarity**

War Comes to Syria

As EARLY AS MARCH 2011, at the very onset of unrest, Fr. Paolo had his residence permit revoked by the authorities. Later in November that same year, the Catholic Church received a letter from the Ministry of Foreign Affairs stating that Fr. Paolo needed to leave Syria. By June 2012, he was being urged by his religious superiors to flee the country over genuine fears for his safety.

Weeks after being expelled, he gave an interview to *Al Arabiya* in Lebanon, where he candidly stated that he had left against his will, defiantly vowing to return.[1] Fr. Paolo believed in the healing power of reconciliation and catharsis. Everyone was capable of redemption; everyone could be rehabilitated under the right circumstances. During the exchange, he tells the story of an impromptu visit from some rather different guests to Mar Musa.

The Visit[2]

February 22, 2012

> On a bright wind-swept day, just after dawn when temperatures were at their lowest, when the wind bit and the tempestuous blaze of summer seemed but a distant memory, they arrived at the base of the monastery. Deir

---

1. Dall'Oglio, "Interview on Al Arabiya," 01:00–03:00.

2. This story is partially recounted by Fr. Paolo during an interview in Lebanon soon after leaving Syria. (Dall'Oglio, "Interview on Al Arabiya," 17:00–18:30.)

Mar Musa perches majestically atop the lofty stone towers that loom over the mars-like orange vista of this part of Southern Syria. A rocky throne of monasticism. The men, all in civilian clothes, wore masks and scarves around their faces. A tour of the ancient site with its fine Christian artwork was not something that interested them.

With labored breath, they slowly climbed, in unison, the steep stone steps that wound their way precipitously to the entrance. Fr. Paolo was the intended recipient of their visit. They had some questions for him. People had been talking and unfounded rumors recirculating that the Community were stashing weapons for rebel forces. Some thought Fr. Paolo's political dissent needed to be tempered.

He had made this isolated outpost into what it was today, painstakingly raising the money himself for its exterior renovation, as well as that of the beautiful frescoes and mosaics of its stone chapel. He had transformed this barren and lonely outpost cradled deep in the bosom of the Anti-Lebanon mountains from an abandoned ruin into the pulsing heart of an intercultural center whose humble buildings welcomed, without judgment, all religions, sects, and nationalities across the region. Since the unrest that was now sweeping the country, it had doubled as a place of refuge, of respite, from the brutality of the security forces, the rag-tag militias, the hoodlums. The men approached Mar Musa's heavy metal door with rapid movements.

As they knocked, the sound reverberated off the surrounding rock with a numb finality. A small nun opened the door and greeted the masked men kindly. Without flinching, Sister Friederike told them that it was rather early for a visit, but that Fr. Paolo was off milking the goats anyway, gesturing toward the top of the mountain.

An hour later Fr. Paolo returned with his pails of milk. He wore the simple clothes of the local workers, a belt fixed around his waist, and a red and white *keffiyeh* wrapped around his greying head to shield from the early morning cold. His face was round, cherubic almost, his pebble-dash hairline receding, and his blue eyes a resolute intent. He was a large man with a presence—girthy, stout, unavoidable. His hands were almost numb from the frosty air, exposed for too long during his milking session. "Why can't I remember to bring damn gloves?" he thought lightheartedly to himself as he descended the stone steps to the monastery, frantically blowing his near-frost-bitten hands for respite. His eyes darted around the scene at the enormous pile of heavy-duty army-issue boots that stood flung at the entrance to the common area.

"A tour from Damascus this early?" he said with a wry thin smile. He shifted uneasily as he made his way to the entrance, his long tunic's black fabric fluttering in the morning breeze. There was a rumbling noise coming from inside. The hum of chatter. As he slowly pushed aside the door, he happened upon the scene. There in the common area of the monastery, surrounded by several monks and nuns, was a large group of militiamen, not only with their footwear removed, but their masks and scarves cast aside too. The weapons had been piled in the corner and the men were on the ground, legs folded contentedly beneath themselves, eating flatbreads and olives unselfconsciously. Sister Friederike had cordially invited them for some tea and a bite of breakfast. She had insisted that Fr. Paolo wouldn't be too long, if they would only be so kind as to wait.

Now, they were engaged in a rather spirited yet absurd discussion with the religious clergy that had gathered curiously around them. They were arguing about the philosophical conundrum of which side of Syrian flatbread—also commonly called *man'oushe*—could be regarded as the right-side up. Which was the bottom and which was the top? Everyone had their own theory. Fr. Paolo had his own view, and waited in anticipation for a lull in the conversation to pipe in, reveling in the boisterous atmosphere.

For Fr. Paolo and the rest of the Community, it was about listening, talking, forgiveness, and—most importantly—love. These pro-government militias had earned an infamous reputation in the months previously for spearheading attacks across

Syria, torturing and murdering—mostly Sunni Syrians—with extra-judicial abandon. They also ensured Shia neighbors stayed away from dangerous protests where live fire was common. They were cynically ratcheting up the sectarian dimension of unrest in the country as a way to persuade religious minorities to support the government. This was in the early days, before the country descended into total madness, and the foreign jihadists hijacked a mostly peaceful, anti-government pro-democracy movement that wanted reform stemming from economic hardship; before a once great country was sacrificed on the altar of barbarism, international proxy interests, and religious extremism.

Even then, Fr. Paolo had predicted with ominous accuracy where Syria was heading. A murderous civil war was the vacuum that this perverted radicalism and its heinous crimes would thrive in. As things lurched toward a spiral of bloodshed that would last years, he unequivocally urged an end to the violence, insisting that negotiation was the only way forward. There could be no other way.

During that same interview in Lebanon, referencing the visit of pro-government radical elements to the monastery, he remarked:

> "These people involved in extremist groups are our children, they do not come from another planet, we have a moral obligation to rehabilitate them, get them out of this cycle and into interreligious care, until they can be reintroduced into society. In Mar Musa, they suddenly found themselves in a different world and their humanity began to surface. These are *our* people and we can get them back on track."[3]

This would not be the last visit of militias to Mar Musa but on this occasion they had been transported, as if by some magic trick, to a different world. A world far away from the carnage that was playing out across the rest of Syria. They had reconnected. An innocent Sister's kind eyes and a casual invitation, looked like it had temporarily disarmed the armed.

3. Dall'Oglio, "Interview on Al Arabiya," 18:00–19:00.

During this time, local people were united through reconstruction projects and rallied to help their fellow neighbors in need. Mar Musa's dismantling of local religious barriers was pivotal when Syrian society began to unravel from 2011. Fear of the unknown, the *other*, was just another weapon used to divide people.

The government were quick to raise the false flag of sectarianism when met with grassroots protests, "non-violent and secular,"[4] that challenged Damascus' autocratic rule and pleaded for long awaited reforms. The small concessions asked for would have made a significant difference to Syrians' lives—more civil liberties, political pluralism, less far-reaching powers for the security services etc. Marchers in the city of Banyas chanted "peaceful, peaceful (. . .) neither Alawite nor Sunni, we want national unity."[5] Sadly, internal and external forces had other plans.

Prof. Szanto believes that the beginnings of the civil war had primarily an economic basis. "Sectarian issues weren't at the very root of the cause," says Szanto. "They [the regime] tried to control religion and also blame it at the same time when it suited them. They learned a lesson from Iraq. They said: 'we will protect the minorities.'"[6] After 2007, Syria became poorer. The price of gasoline tripled, Iraqi refugees flooded in. People were resentful, blamed the government, and then an element of anti-Shia sentiment became evident. Services were stretched and people relied more on their families which strengthened family and tribal ties. The Israel–Lebanon war in 2006 also played a part. Syria absorbed up to one million refugees, putting a huge strain on accommodation, services, and infrastructure.[7]

Yet that is not the full story. Before the war, the sectarian dimension between different religious creeds and denominations in Syria was palpable. The ruling Alawites had their own dialect and a very clear accent—even though they spoke Arabic. Subsequently, they were easily identifiable. On hearing the accent, people

4. Erlich, *Inside Syria,* 83.

5. Bartkowski and Kahf in Erlich, *Inside Syria,* 83.

6. Szanto, Interview.

7. Szanto, Interview.

immediately became guarded, alert. They would think to themselves, "Are they working for the government, the *Mukhabarat*, the *Shabiha*[8]?"[9] In this way, even language could divide and sow mistrust and doubt. "Before the war mixed-religion families were rare," states Shady Hamadi. "Even then you could still feel the sectarian dimension of society between different religious creeds and denominations in Syria."[10]

It is important not to downplay this sectarian element. "When I first went to Syria as a young student in the late 1990s, village women wore headscarves, but it was unusual to see urban women in hijab," says Prof. Loosley, who worked alongside Fr. Paolo in Syria for three years. "By 2010, the hijab was commonplace and more women were wearing the abaya—incredibly rare before."[11] She maintains that this societal sea-change all stemmed from growing anti-Western views post 9/11, as well as Saudi money pouring into Syria funding Wahhabi mosques and stirring up Sunni discontent. The genius of the Ba'athists was to latch onto this and use it as a pretext for their own political purposes.

A combination of these factors fomented discontent and created the optimal conditions where even the smallest incident could ignite the dry tinderbox of the country's frustrations. Renowned reporter and journalist Robert Fisk, who was in Syria in April 2011, reported that "The Syrian Ministry of the Interior was playing the sectarian card again yesterday; the protesters were sectarian, they claimed."[12] However, it transpired that both sides were egregiously exploiting sectarian division.

At the onset of the uprising in Syria, the government were appealing to minority groups—Christians particularly, who up

8. The *Shabiha* or *Shabeeha* were smuggling outfits before 2011; during the war they became state sponsored militias of the Syrian government with a terrible reputation for thuggish brutality. Their name is connected to the word *Shabha* and translates as "ghosts." (Yassin-Kassab and Al-Shami, *Burning Country,* 47.)

9. Hamadi, Interview.

10. Hamadi, Interview.

11. Loosley, Interview.

12. Fisk, "Every Concession," line 19–20.

to that point had always felt safe in Syria—cajoling them into staying loyal to the government. Assad was positioning himself as the only guarantor of the well-being and security of religious minorities. Thus, the regime calculatedly strove to divide and discredit the opposition by instilling fear in large sections of society along explicitly religious lines. Robert Fisk wrote in October 2011, "a sectarian war may well be in the cynical interests of any regime fighting for its life."[13]

However, it is obvious that Assad did not have a monopoly on the exploitation of religion differences for more nefarious political ends; the opposition were also involved in similar antics. While not at the root of the unrest, the specter of sectarianism was undoubtedly being wielded by both sides as violence intensified. *The Independent* reported of rebel forces in 2011, "In the village of Hala, Christian shops are shut as their owners contemplate what are clearly sectarian demands to join in the uprising against Assad."[14] Fr. Paolo saw through the smokescreen of sectarianism, knowing the inherent peril of any society pulled apart along religious fissures, once declaring "The myth that all Alawites are with the regime has to be eradicated. It is awful."[15] Mar Musa's inclusive message of inter-religious tolerance, respect, and trust, was the very antithesis of this callous manipulation of social, ethnic, and religious differences. He knew how easily these fault lines could be prized open, and strove vehemently to push back against it.

The Community's IFD at Mar Musa and beyond, played a vital part in exposing a large section of society to other religions and helping them move forward without being shackled by mistrust, prejudice, and fear of the *other*. As religious leaders were also involved in initiatives, it sent a message of validation to their congregation that dialogue *was* a positive thing and most importantly, not to fear it.

While not always surrounded by ideal political circumstances for openly expressing religious and social views, the monks and

13. Fisk, "Syria Slips," line 24.
14. Fisk, "Out of Syria's Darkness," line 23–25.
15. Dall'Oglio, "Interview on Al Arabiya," 16:00.

nuns circumvented this limitation by facilitating "a real relationship between different religious groups built on knowledge, shared experience, and contact."[16] Most crucially, Mar Musa offered a nonjudgmental and open space for people to dispel backward ideas about the religious *other* which might have been passed down via locals', family members', or peers' limited experiences. Insular ideas that could later be exploited to turn neighbor against neighbor by more malign actors with their own agendas.

Even in the face of growing unrest, Fr. Paolo remained committed to reconciliation. The people in the villages around Mar Musa were able to build and foster permanent meaningful relationships with their neighbors across other faiths. Fr. Paolo once said of Mar Musa that it was his life's ambition "to attract people to a spiritual atmosphere of friendship, hospitality, consideration, respect. In a word, love."[17] This might be Mar Musa's single greatest accomplishment. They demonstrated that it was possible to coexist in a region where religious division, tension, and manipulation, were encroaching year by year.

Fr. Paolo was unequivocal, once exclaiming, "I am not prepared or interested to live in a world that does not put hospitality or cooperation, brotherhood, solidarity, at the center of community life,"[18] and to this principle he stood resolute. Al-Khalil and Mar Musa was an island of brotherly love that transcended religious categorization, encircled by a seething ocean of instability. Ironically, as so happened, that encroachment was closer than any of them could have ever thought.

Not Suited for Silence: Exile and Activism

As events unraveled in 2011 and the poison of civil war slowly seeped into Syrian society, massacres against civilians were mounting and the church—in Syria and abroad—remained

16. Bashir, Interview.

17. COSV, "Deir Mar Musa Documentary," 5:45–6:25.

18. Bashir, Interview.

silent, understandably fearing for the safety of their congregations living in a predominantly Muslim country in the throes of a Sunni revolt.

Fr. Paolo's was a lone shrill voice of dissent and criticism—even more direct and outspoken than usual—silence for him was deafening complicity, once famously stating, "Words force their way out of me and keep flowing. I am not suited for silence."[19] Through it all, he fervently believed that democracy was still feasible in Syria, "but only if freedom of expression is assured and you waive any attack on human dignity and abuses against human rights."[20] There was only one side of history he wanted to be on: that of the protestors, the oppressed, the downtrodden. His self-professed mission at this time was to unite the Syrian opposition and participate in a constitutional process toward democracy.

The people had rallied with gusto around the pebbledash-bearded, charismatic Italian, a man already very well-liked in religiously diverse Syria and known for his pluralist IFD efforts in Mar Musa. They affectionately called him *Abuna Paolo*.[21] Here was a Christian man of the cloth who was not shy in telling the truth and who somehow represented every facet of Syrian society: Christians, Muslims, Druze, etc. He was a magnet for the opposition.

Then a curious thing happened—spontaneously. The people who were protesting peacefully on the streets in the early days, those who bravely faced down Assad's sharp shooters, dedicated a march to Fr. Paolo. People in the streets were marching against the government with *his* image held in front of them—Damascus. Hama. Aleppo. The people needed a symbol. He was a reminder of the famous Christian politician, Fares al-Khoury,[22] who, like Fr.

---

19. Dall'Oglio. "Interview on Al Arabiya," 05:00–06:00.

20. Falciatori, "Who is Father Dall'Oglio," line 1–2.

21. Bashir, Interview.

22. During the French occupation in Syria, al-Khoury, a Christian, was going into mosques and praying. People had never seen this before. He was a clear and bright symbol of unity and he later became prime minister of Syria. (Hamadi, Interview.)

Paolo, was also a potent symbol of what Syria could be: a country for everyone. [23]

Paolo had become a figurehead for the opposition as he had given a voice to the voiceless. He stood with them, in the name of human rights and of their legitimate aspirations for freedom and a loosening of the Ba'athist noose of surveillance and repression. The march was to reiterate how religion could unite—not divide.

Kofi Annan presented his Syrian Peace Plan to the UN Security Council on 16 March 2012. It required the Syrian government "address the legitimate aspirations and concerns of the Syrian people."[24] Hope hung in the air by a thread. Tragically, the doomed peace plan was never taken seriously—by any of the sides involved. In May, a furious Fr. Paolo sent an open letter to the Secretary General pleading for intervention and a no-fly zone to protect the people whose blood by now covered the streets. He railed against their hesitation, roaring, "The country is drowning, there can be no more silence."[25]

Just one month later, the UN mission to Syria would pull out; in June 2012, Fr. Paolo would leave his beloved Syria after receiving a letter from the religious authorities via Damascus. They urged him to flee the country for his own safety. Soon after passing the reins of leadership to Sister Houda in Mar Musa, he said he was depressed but hardly surprised by the decision.[26] Irrespective, one facet of his life remained unchanged: he was determined to continue the work of "dialogue and negotiation" which Syria was in "dire need of,"[27]—outside the country.

Writer, activist, and close friend of Fr. Paolo, Gianluca Solera, states, "Paolo knew it wasn't just about Syria. It was about the principle of self-determination. About people's dignity. About the idea of democracy in the world. He knew what was at stake

23. Hamadi, Interview.

24. Annan, "Syria Peace Plan."

25. Dall'Oglio, "Interview on Al Arabiya," 06:00.

26. Dall'Oglio, "Interview on Al Arabiya," 01:30–02:00.

27. Dall'Oglio, "Interview on Al Arabiya," 21:00–25:00.

and what could happen if this conflict developed and radicalization occurred."[28]

His political involvement, frankness, and outspoken support for the opposition were unquestionably problematic for the church—inside and outside Syria. He had even sent a letter to Pope Francis before being expelled, although its desperate call went unanswered.[29] After sneaking back into Syria in 2013, he wrote from deep inside rebel-controlled territory of his profound sense of frustration and abandonment at the Vatican's procrastination.

On another occasion, he was openly unapologetic, almost taking a devilish glee in toying with official church protocol. "In religions there are certain rules," he insisted. "A free person who speaks freely is a nuisance. Reconciliation is our future and we are committed to it. There can be no reconciliation without a mature democracy, without freedom of opinion, without true humanity."[30]

The hesitation of the church in Syria to condemn the killing simply confirmed for him what he had always suspected: the Syrian religious authorities were very much in the pockets of the state. He loudly berated their unbending political fence-sitting. He had always insisted that if push came to shove, they "would not say a word without permission."[31] They were proving him right.

Fr. Paolo was far from a shrewd political analyst. His talents lay elsewhere. Some of his requests, such as 50,000 UN observers on the ground to live with the people, attend demonstrations, to be a visible international civic community on the ground in Syria standing side by side with Syrians,[32] were simply impractical and too far-fetched to be ever realistically achievable in the tightly-controlled sectarian morass of Assad's Syria. The Syrian leader had become even more mendacious and paranoid in the face of deteriorating security across large swathes of the country; that and mounting international pressure to concede to demands meant

28. Solera, Interview.

29. Solera, Interview.

30. Dall'Oglio, "Interview on Al Arabiya," 24:00.

31. Dall'Oglio, "Interview on Al Arabiya," 22:00–25:00.

32. Dall'Oglio, "Interview on Al Arabiya," 12:00.

that slackening the reins of authority was never a likely option. Assad's was a siege mentality.

Syrian political analyst, KM Alam, recalls the political naïveté of Fr. Paolo's plan. "This is too idealistic. It's Syria. It lies between three war zones. Multiple intelligence agencies are involved. It's too simplistic to think that you can bring these people in from outside to mediate a very complex situation. It simply wouldn't work."[33]

During exile, Fr. Paolo spent his time in Lebanon, Deir Maryam al-Adhra monastery in Sulaymaniyah, Iraq, and at various awareness-raising events advocating for Syrian democracy in Belgium, France, and Italy. His was an inextinguishable fire that burned for the Syrian people and their freedom. He was a vociferous advocate for the opposition. "He was not shy. He became like a diplomat after leaving Syria. He gave voice to the people," confirms Solera. "He believed his mission was to explain to those far away from the turmoil, the reality on the ground in Syria. He [Fr. Paolo] embraced this role."[34]

Fr. Paolo had always been a firm believer in the power of non-violent resistance and dialogue. In early 2013, he re-entered Syria on a clandestine mission to visit Free Syrian Army-controlled areas and talk to people there. An online journal he kept at the time reveals the most unlikely of priestly activities in this war zone. He describes himself and his accompaniers recording two TV broadcasts for a pro-rebel Free Syrian Army TV station.[35] The extrovert in him was enjoying the limelight, but, in doing so, he was inadvertently raising his balding head above the parapet where more unscrupulous Islamic actors would soon be joining the fray. He was moving about the country in mainly FSA-controlled areas with often deteriorating security. His online journal portrays, with cool indifference, his nonchalance in the ever-present face of real and immediate danger.

33. Alam, Interview.

34. Solera, Interview.

35. Dall'Oglio, "Syrian Diaries," 2013.

Shards of Iron and Fire [36]

Today is February 26 2013. As we are recording two TV broadcasts for a pro-rebel FSA (Free Syrian Army) TV station, there is a deafening cacophony of shots, along with loud explosions and short pounding bangs of intensity that make our ears ring and our heads ache. One of the neighborhoods we visit has been utterly devastated. Ripped apart and disemboweled. The carnage of a bomb exploding in a densely built-up urban area is like an active volcano, its belly filled with shrapnel and chemicals, spewing forth, without warning, a torrent of ash and debris. It flattens everything in its path, indiscriminately. Having studied under the shadow of mighty Vesuvius, how odd that this comes to my mind here, hundreds of miles away in the Levant. The bombs are called *faraghiya* by the locals. You would know them as Barrel Bombs. The Americans and Israelis were first to use them. Now they have become the affordable and highly effective weapon of choice for Assad's regime. The fact that they are quite inaccurate is irrelevant. Usually helicopters launch them at high altitudes on rebel-controlled areas. Whirring, whirling, death-delivery machines. The destruction they wreak is immense—packed with up to a ton of explosives and other material of questionable origin. Such is the cruel nature of conflict, civilians mostly pay the cost, at least those unlucky enough to be living in rebel/FSA-controlled areas.

Nubl and al-Zahraa, north of Aleppo and near the Turkish Border, are predominately Shia towns surrounded by Sunni villages. They have been under siege here by fighters from the Free Syrian Army since July 2012. Before the war, local relations were convivial, but now there is nothing but suspicion. How quickly this mistrust metastasized, turning neighbor against neighbor. Kidnappings have become common between the various tribes and religious groups. There seems a pressing need

---

36. What follows is a creative non-fiction account of Fr. Paolo's journey around rebel enclaves of Syria at war in February and March of 2013, after his expulsion from the country in June 2012. It is based on his own journal accounts. (Dall'Oglio, "Syrian Diaries.")

to remove the government forces from these areas and liberate them, for they want to be liberated, but we need to do it without massacre, without slaughter. I wonder if that is even possible anymore? Things are starting to spiral. How long do we have before it totally unravels? I pray for a quick resolution and an end to this fighting. I try to remain positive despite the reality on the ground.

We leave under cover of darkness to bring a crew member to the relative safety of the Turkish border. It's bitterly cold and the wind numbs us, tearing at our exposed skin, revealing our rumbling stomachs and sunken eyes. We need to arrive before the border closes. Time is short. Our car breaks down three times due to the improvised diesel now on offer throughout much of "Free Syria." Who knows what it really contains? Coughing and spluttering, like a wheezing asthmatic, it is hardly reassuring. Driving back, the night's silence and jet blackness enveloping us completely, our car's headlights suddenly illuminate another vehicle ahead, in the shadows on the shoulder of the road, eerily tilted on its side. It sits there comically but on approaching there is the stench of death. We realize it is a smoldering shell, twisted and mutilated, like the four charred bodies still sitting upright inside it. Free Syrian Army soldiers caught unawares by a missile strike. A quick but unromantic death.

We drive westwards to a mountainous area where the Orontes river crosses into Turkey. Again there are more problems with our car. We really don't want to end up stranded here! Later, we approach Darkush near Idlib—a Sunni and Christian enclave that stretches down to the Mediterranean coast of Latakia. We are received with incredible hospitality by our Sunni hosts, who are friends of one of the journalists in our group. They tell us that the Alawites, who once lived in this area, have all since fled as government forces went into retreat. Displaced Sunni families from other government-controlled areas have already taken their place. And so the perverse merry-go-round of this war plays out and the human cost mounts. Our kind hosts empathize with the plight of anyone who must move their family at great risk. Many here wear the psychological burden of fear and repression on their haunted faces, their eyes always somewhere else. I am terribly unsettled at seeing this anguish among people that I have such affection for.

In the morning as we cross the river, the sound of machine gun fire echoes out in front of us menacingly, and some regime shells land worryingly close to our convoy. You can smell the fear in the group. I am taken back to my time in Lebanon in the late seventies, early eighties. I swear unapologetically as one detonation catches me unawares, "Taking the LORD's name in vain again, Paolo!—hardly a good role model these days?" I mumble to myself.

We pass mountain valleys that are heavy with the blossom of spring flowers, the lushness of the soil readying itself for another season of growth. The flowers are particularly beautiful this year after an unusually rainy winter. Taftanaz military airport has seen some of the fiercest fighting and it looks it. The withered watchtower on the perimeter of the airstrip has collapsed, like a broken asphalt candle. Large craters pockmark the landing strip indiscriminately, the dry concrete is cracked and chapped. It is pathetic and forlorn—a hazard for the most skilled pilot to land anything on its cratered surface. A few kilometers away, there is seldom a home to be seen that has escaped damage. But already life is stirring as the irrepressible local people move about, trying to piece together their previous lives.

In Saraqeb, another rebel held township, our colleagues anxiously fidget about and eventually leave in distress. I don't blame them. The aerial bombardment is all around us. There is a disquieting yet welcoming calm in between blasts; the city has been all but deserted, abandoned to its fate, whatever that may be. There is little doubt that the rebels have limited weapons and ammunition. Their guns do little to combat the aerial threat. Just yesterday, 13 rebels died trying to open a passage for much needed supplies. The government try to choke their efforts. The anti-aircraft station that I am shown looks like something that belongs in a First World War museum, not here in a battle raging in 2013. It is a depressing symbol of the insurgency's impotency. All its limitations laid bare and exposed.

Later that day, I am the guest of an Islamic brigade who have taken over the area and seem to be working with the FSA. Not only have jihadists ruined beards the world over, but here it is interesting to note that the level of radicalism can be measured by their tendency to smoke openly or not. For example, the Salafist-leaning *Jabhat al-Nusra* completely ban smoking and severely admonish members who are caught doing it—however secretly. Some of these guys look funny, like caricature villains with their enormous bushy manes of wiry black hair and bulbous hooked noses. Young men most of this crew, with mothers who pine for them back home. Wherever that is.

We bumped into a brigade of *al-Nusra*,[37] and they were always keen to talk to us. We even engaged in discussion about interreligious and political matters. It was all rather pleasant and well-mannered. They were thankful that the West hadn't yet intervened in Syria as it gave the Islamists a chance to get a foothold, they maintained. One officer proudly bellowed at me, "Syria will be the beginning of the liberation of the whole Muslim world!" I wondered if their plan also involved free and fair elections and a Syria that functions for all Syrians?

Most of the Islamic fighters I have encountered here are Syrian, as are their companions and supporters. Tomorrow I want to go south but there is a chance the FSA will not let me through. They say it is too much of a risk. The dangers increase by the day. I am overwhelmed by their hospitality, for it seems they are genuinely concerned for my well-being. They even say they love me.

My hosts this evening seem more easy-going than the anti-smoking brigade and only forbid smoking in public. Reassuringly, as is the case with more pious religious folk, appearances are more important than any

37. Also known as the *al-Nusra Front* or *Jabhat al-Nusra*. They were anti-government jihadists with a Salafist ideology aiming to overthrow Assad and form an Islamist state. They were some of the most effective rebel forces fighting in Syria at this time and seen as more moderate than the likes of *Daesh*.

strict doctrine. Outside of this communal space, you can do as you wish. Thank God indeed! I am dying for a smoke. That first hit of nicotine, like everything, even more appealing when it is illicit. I pop into one of the rooms which houses their satellite communication and computer systems, and light up, pulling on the filter greedily, the billowing smoke filling the compact space, stuffed with wires and gadgets, in moments. It feels so good as I sit on their thick carpet and rest my head on the bare stone wall.

The room I sleep in is very well heated against the chill of early Spring nights by a handcrafted green Aleppo stove. What a piece of equipment! Here you simply take a blanket and lie down where you want. The level of cleanliness of these guys is remarkable. Their mothers taught them well. You could eat your dinner off the floor I sleep on—if there was a dinner to eat. Some bread will do for now.

In Rome they hesitate, but Syria is all shards of iron and fire. In the city of Al-Tamanah, whose inhabitants have long since fled, the battle-front is on the main road into town. Assad wants to stop the supply of humanitarian aid and its distribution along this crucial transport artery. Trucks of cargo have been stuck here for days— frozen but rotting in the glaring sun. The aid's recipients getting hungrier and hungrier while I get angrier. Fools! How can they do this to their own people—to fellow Syrians?

There is now an ever-pressing need to open up a guaranteed humanitarian aid corridor that must be respected by both sides. Much needed supplies for civilians must get in. The time for deliberation is over. After the last few days, I am incredibly concerned about the deteriorating situation across significant tracts of the country. Unity is being eroded on the rebel side. There are worrying stories circulating that some more extreme Islamist factions are shooting first and asking questions later. It's easy to kill the wrong person in a war that is becoming increasingly complex, with a multitude of rebel groups vying for territorial supremacy in certain key areas—all of them with various ideological differences;

that and pro-government support, including training and weapons, pouring in from Russians, Iranians, Lebanese, and Iraqi Shiite is also turning out to be a decisive factor in tilting an evenly balanced stalemate.

The safety of the civilian population must be the overarching priority now, along with the reestablishment of law and order. The current Islamization of the battle is irrefutable and must be taken into account. It is imperative that Christians separate themselves from Assad, and become proactive in striving for a new democracy in the country. Christian leaders in Syria say nothing, but Syrian Christians must not be swayed by pro-government rhetoric and fear-mongering.

Vanishing

Fr. Paolo tried his hand at negotiating the release of hostages held by an Islamic brigade in Homs before leaving Syria. He was already starting to become more reckless, impervious to the inherent risk. He intimated that it was somehow his duty and he seemed darkly curious about his fate. Compelled by the pain of the family for their missing relatives, his sense of compassion was overriding. "I had been wearing the hat of Islamic/Christian religious dialogue for years," he said at the time. "Would it work in reality or not? Is it simply theoretical or practical? So I went to al-Kusair to test it."[38] On this occasion he was successful, but it had whetted his appetite for more daring heroics.

He covertly returned to Syria and Al-Raqqah in 2013, during the blazing heat of a July Ramadan. According to sources, Al-Raqqah had become the first city to fall into the hands of the opposition, and they were experimenting with self-government. Disturbingly, at this time, the shadow of *Daesh* was already on the Syrian horizon, and the jihadists were getting a strong foothold in many parts of the east of the country. Fr. Paolo went to Al-Raqqah to negotiate the release of Kurdish colleagues with Islamic brigades, but thereafter details become muddied and what follows is

38. Dall'Oglio, "Interview Al Arabiya," 06:30–07:30.

mere conjecture and rumor. All we really know is that something went wrong. Tragically he is still missing, presumed dead.

Those who knew Fr. Paolo and what was happening in Syria at the time, have various views on his disappearance and its effect on the Community he left behind. A religious colleague, Fr. Zygmunt Kwiatkowski, talks of Fr. Paolo's quest to try to unite the splintering opposition. He states:

> "Fr. Paolo supported the opposition and its military wing—the FSA. After they conquered Al-Raqqah, he was invited as an honorary guest to the city. Suddenly, he was kidnapped by an armed militia, his mobile phone stopped working and email contact stopped (. . .) He was invited to Al-Raqqah as a public guest, not in a private capacity. It was in the public interest to ensure his safety and protect him. Why was there no investigation? Why no attempt to free him? Why did the world never find out what happened?"[39]

The implication remains that the FSA were not entirely in control of the area, symptomatic of a conflict that was becoming ever more complex, involving disparate actors with diverging ideologies, methods, and goals. As a result, it seems, Fr. Paolo paid the ultimate price for his negotiation efforts.

Another account describes a westerner who was in captivity at this time very much resembling Fr. Paolo. The Italian is said to have asked one of his fresh-faced captors how old he was. When the youngster answered that he was in his twenties, Fr. Paolo remarked with typical wry wit and irascible scorn, "I read the Qur'an before you were even born."[40] Apparently, when they came to shoot him there was a physical fight. Other reports said he had been dropped down a hole called "el Huta"—a natural geological formation outside the town, used for the disposal of bodies. The church refuse to say he is dead as they want concrete evidence. For now, it seems they will not get it.

39. Kwiatkowski JR, *Życie Między Pustyniami*, 245.

40. Kociejowski, Interview.

Poet and writer Marius Kociejowski, who spent some time in Mar Musa with Fr. Paolo, has a telling paragraph in his book *Zaroaster's Children*. He chillingly depicts one of the most vivid dreams he ever had in the months immediately following Fr. Paolo's disappearance. It was a time when hope was still fresh. He recalls a black and white world where he and his wife are driving through a remote part of the Syrian countryside, only to find themselves running out of fuel. They pull into the nearest town and the author recalls hearing singing coming from a nearby building. When he enters, the singing stops, and he hears a voice in Arabic that is unmistakable in its raspy, guttural tones. He shouts over the heads of the densely packed crowd:

> "'Father Paolo,' I cried out, 'we are short of petrol and I'm in need of a toilet.'
>
> "There was silence, then an audible ripple in the congregation of someone trying to squeeze through. The figure of Paolo emerged from the wall of people, not the burly man so familiar to me but a skeletal figure, horribly emaciated, his hair grown, beard unruly. It was him and it was *not* him.
>
> 'You are alive!' he exclaimed.
>
> Tears rolled down his cheeks as he embraced me.
>
> 'On the contrary,' I replied, '*you* are alive.'
>
> 'Yes, but it's *your* name on the list of those to be killed.'
>
> I awoke, greatly stricken."[41]

Dilemmas and Ramifications

As Fr. Paolo criticized the government's crackdown on peaceful protestors at the onset of unrest, later he would become more balanced in pleading for restraint from *both* sides. "He would directly criticize the government and rebels if civilians were

41. Kociejowski, *Zaroaster's Children*, 151.

targeted," Fr. Jens explains. "Twice there was a letter issued to all commanders of the Free Syrian Army that they should respect civilians. He was very sharp with them also."[42] The basis of his criticism was always moral.

A question lingers: how had other members of Mar Musa felt about Fr. Paolo's loud and unapologetic criticism of the regime in Damascus when violence began? Was he justified in jeopardizing the safety of his fellow monks and nuns without their explicit consent? Fr. Jens states:

> "He tried to make a difference. When he had to leave the country, he gave the leadership of Mar Musa to Sister Houda. I know he endangered a few groups at certain moments and he was reckless—yes. What was his mindset at that time? I don't know. I do know that when he came back to Syria, there were sometimes wrong decisions made."[43]

Despite those possible wrong decisions, Fr Paolo believed it was worse to do nothing.

Therein lies the dilemma: is it better to stay quiet and let evil prosper, or speak up and do something, even if that might endanger you and those closest to you? No such dilemma tormented Fr. Paolo. All his actions sprung from conscience and the moral principles that underpinned his philosophy. To do nothing in the face of evil, to stay passive when innocents were being slaughtered, was to be complicit in their slaughter. For him, silence facilitated the oppressor, not the oppressed. "If there is something wrong and you can do something, you must do something—there is no choice here," states Fr. Jens, regarding Fr. Paolo's mindset at the time. "It's a moral imperative. How to go about that is another more complex question. He saw a need and he needed to act. There was no other option for him."[44]

After Fr. Paolo left Syria, he visited Deir Maryam al-Adhra in Iraq. Fr. Jens describes him as being in a political frame of mind at

42. Petzold, Interview.

43. Petzold, Interview.

44. Petzold, Interview.

the time, outwardly at least, yet he is quick to insist that the base of his actions was always humanitarian. "He was preoccupied with the issue of Syria descending into a long terrible war and was in political mode,"[45] says Fr. Jens.

Others believe that Fr. Paolo could have been more restrained, particularly as members of his team in Mar Musa may not have appreciated such attention. Initially, the Community may not have agreed with his pro-rebel talk, but were resigned to it anyway. "They were his flock and probably expected it,"[46] Prof. Szanto opines. Yet, his actions may have jeopardized those who did not want to be on the regime radar. "Yes, it endangered people," says old friend of the Community and Fr. Paolo, Prof. Loosley. "If Paolo had just spoken for himself that was one thing, but in Syria he was seen as the founder of the Al-Khalil Community by the authorities—so when he criticized anything, it was taken as being representative of the Community view. He was seen as speaking on their behalf."[47] It was an impulsive streak that was beginning to become more pronounced.

After Fr. Paolo's exile from Syria, he continued his criticism of the government and pleaded for democratic transition. He enjoyed the media attention he was receiving. His moment in the limelight may have appealed to the vanity element in his character, and his more grandiose ambitions. The candid celebrity mode he was in, while travelling around Europe in 2012 and 2013, often irked other Syrians who had to return to the country and deal with the consequences of such flagrant outspokenness.

One such occasion is recalled when Prof. Loosley met Fr. Paolo in Rome, after he had addressed Italian politicians about the fate of Syria. An angry Syrian woman admonished him publically for his impetuousness. "You are not Syrian and you need to be quiet," she said angrily. "You don't get it. Some people have to go back there [Syria]. This all has implications."[48] Her justification for

45. Petzold, Interview.

46. Szanto, Interview.

47. Loosley, Interview.

48. Loosley, Interview.

lambasting him was that his actions could have a knock-on effect for her family and friends who had to live in Syria. She had a point. "Europeans write from the safety of their homes—extolling Paolo as a champion of human rights and freedom. Syrians don't always agree," Prof Loosley explains. "My sympathies lie with the Syrians because they cannot afford to be idealistic like Europeans. They have to live with the daily consequences of this war.

Prof. Loosley was annoyed and upset with Fr. Paolo on finding out he had been kidnapped. "I felt he had placed his own personal and religious beliefs ahead of their [the Community's] needs. The Community was his child, and in that parental role I felt he should have sacrificed this other urge for the sake of their greater good."

It also becomes evident that Fr. Paolo's devil-may-care actions may have endangered his legacy and that of the Community he founded. "My personal feeling is that in the long-term the Community of Al-Khalil is his most important legacy and that is now at risk. For that reason I don't think Paolo did the right thing," Prof. Loosley states without sentimentality. "His first duty was to the Community and I don't think that he fully considered what would happen to them."[49] She felt strongly that he should have taken more account of the impact of his actions.

Fr. Paolo was a bombastic and flamboyant character in the truest sense of the word, equal parts visionary and dreamer. He offended and delighted with equal aplomb, and his charm often salvaged potential disasters. He was overly ambitious with his expansionist plans for the Community, given their limited resources. "You have to temper ambition with realism. Grandiose dreams are nice to have, whether they are feasible or the right way forward remains to be seen,"[50] states Prof. Loosley. He was slippery to define, paradoxical elements of both ego and self-effacement complicating an already complex character. Yet, there is little doubt that he achieved what he did *because* of these qualities, not despite them. It was not only Catholic churches in the East who were irritated

49. Loosley, Interview.
50. Loosley, Interview.

by him, Orthodox and Melkite also had their doubts. His bullish nature and propensity to ridicule the establishment went so far against the grain, the hierarchy could simply not reconcile it.

Yes, there were plenty of flaws, but he had a shrewd awareness of his own limitations. "I greatly admired him but he was a vain man. He even said so himself," says writer and poet Marius Kociejowski. "Vanity was the one thing he had yet to conquer. It made him too confident."[51] It would be all too easy to paint Fr. Paolo as simply anti-establishment, the cocky maverick, but that is too simplistic, his character was much more nuanced than that. He desperately wanted to change things but was conscious of his own limitations. "I think Paolo being the outsider and dissident could be too easily exaggerated," Kociejowski elaborates. "He knew he was a member of an order, and he wanted to abide by its rules, but he also wanted dialogue and change."[52] Doing anything in a country such as Syria was incredibly difficult, yet he somehow managed to overcome these obstacles, year in year out, against the odds. His achievements were remarkable in many respects.

Fr. Paolo made an instant connection with so many people. Perhaps they saw their own weaknesses and failings in him? We are all imperfect in some way and he was certainly no angel. "He was a man of many flaws," says Kociejowski. "He was a remarkable figure who needs to be both honored and criticized in the right way."[53]

The immense affinity that the man had among Muslims is testament to the success of his interreligious dialogue efforts. "By and large he was incredibly well-liked by Muslims. I know he would go to Damascus in his monk's robes and sandals, and he was a very welcome figure, everyone knew him, he was so popular,"[54] explains Kociejowski, remembering Fr. Paolo's huge rapport with the Muslim community. He masterfully mediated for both sides, effortlessly crossing the religious divide, but during the war it was

51. Kociejowski, Interview.
52. Kociejowski, Interview.
53. Kociejowski, Interview.
54. Kociejowski, Interview.

a different Syria. He thought no one would ever harm him and he was immune to the threat. He went too far.

Quiet Heroes

Fr. Paolo's pioneering IFD and peace work continues with many taking up the mantle. Other priests, monks, and nuns, silently work on projects without the media presence that Fr. Paolo commanded and the attention he so enjoyed. Many chose to stay and continue their work, despite the ever-present threats to their safety.

Fr. Jacques Mourad, co-founder of Mar Musa and the Community of Al-Khalil back in 1991, had his own towering accomplishments in Mar Elian monastery in Al-Qaryatayn. His efforts at everyday dialogue between members of his own local community included various rebuilding projects and initiatives to provide shelter for displaced families during the fighting. He resolutely remained with his parishioners, and was eventually kidnapped and tortured by *Daesh* in 2015, only to be luckily rescued five months later.[55]

Fr. Jens' soothing words to his parishioners as the scourge of *Daesh* encroached on their Community in Sulaymaniyah, Iraq, in 2014. "He understood if people had to leave for family reasons etc.," recalls Prof. Szanto. "For those who wanted to stay, he said that it was also important to bear witness. That was calming and consoling at a very traumatic time."[56]

Fr. Youssef, fellow monk and colleague of Fr. Paolo, who, according to colleague Zygmunt Kwiatkowski, boldly negotiated truces between government and rebel forces during periods of escalation in the town of Al-Qaryatayn. He was almost killed in an attack on Al-Khalil's sister monastery—Mar Elian. He was fortunate to escape under heavy fire.[57] Of his decision to stay on in an area that was becoming increasingly unstable, and any talk of bravery, he said:

55. Gagliarduci, "In Syrian Monastery Priest who escaped," lines 9–11.

56. Szanto, Interview.

57. Kwiatkowski JR, *Życie Między Pustyniami*, 245–255.

"We as a Community are not courageous for it is our choice to stay in solidarity. We were ready to leave and had our things packed in case there was an emergency and we had to suddenly flee. We didn't stay to be heroes. We stayed to do God's will."[58]

Others have sadly not been so fortunate. There was the selflessness of Dutch Jesuit monk Fr. Frans van der Lugt from Homs. He had been responsible for undertaking spiritual retreats called *Masir* in the Syrian countryside around Mar Musa with local youth from the area. He had been in Syria since 1966. He had set up a community center and farm called *Al-Ard* just outside the city of Homs in 1980. It had a vineyard and lush gardens mostly run by disabled people from the area. The center was also known as a place of dialogue between Muslims and Christians.

He fearlessly stayed on after the February 2014 evacuation deadline in Homs. Fr. Frans said of his decision to remain:

"The Syrian people have given me so much, so much kindness, inspiration, and everything they have. If the Syrian people are suffering now, I want to share their pain and their difficulties."[59]

He was executed by *Al-Nusra* in the following weeks.

Legacy: A Final Reminisce

The question of martyrdom and Fr. Paolo's cavalier attitude to risk is worth examining. Why was he blindly putting himself in such peril? It raises the question of the paradoxical nature of modern-day moral leadership and all that can be lost from following its call. Fr. Paolo, a well-known Christian religious figure in the region, knew the inherent danger involved in interaction with unsavory extremist factions. His actions in Al-Raqqah, after secretly returning to Syria, belied any sense of rationale and common sense. Mere months previously, Boulos Yaziji, who led the Greek Orthodox

58. Youssef, Interview.
59. Mass, "Jesuit Priest Murdered," lines 24–25.

Church in Aleppo, and Yohanna Ibrahim, head of the Syriac Orthodox Church in the city, were kidnapped by militants, sending shockwaves through the religious communities of the region. The capture of prominent church figures was good business and could pull in hefty ransom payments for their jailers. The "lucky" ones were kidnapped, tortured, and eventually released.

Surely charismatic figures like Fr. Paolo are more effective alive—convincing, antagonizing, cajoling, roaring? Solera states with a tone of fatalistic resignation, "I am afraid he is dead. The destiny of Fr. Paolo was to challenge contemporary institutions—the establishment. Many people have unfortunately died for their beliefs. That is life."[60]

Prof. Loosley explains how Fr. Paolo's propensity for placing himself in dangerous situations could be seen as naïve—even foolish—for it spectacularly back-fired:

> "Fr. Jacques' [Mar Elian] difficulty with *Daesh* was accidental. He was in the wrong place at the wrong time and for that he had to endure so much, i.e., what he went through physically and mentally after his kidnapping at their hands. There is so much sympathy for Fr. Jacques, but Fr. Paolo put *himself* in harm's way to prove a point. That's really hard to reconcile when you know someone. I loved Paolo dearly as a friend but still disagreed with some of his actions."[61]

Here one can draw parallels with the fate of Fr. Frans from Homs—yet there remain striking differences, according to Prof. Loosley:

> "They [Fr. Paolo and Fr. Frans] both had the same love for Syrians, and the same idea about setting up communities that would help the Syrian people. When the war started, they both had the same choice: how would they live their lives and support their respective communities? Paolo thought his choice was to leave, but Fr. Frans chose to stay and defend his community until he was eventually

60. Solera, Interview.
61. Loosley, Interview.

murdered. In this case I have more understanding of Fr. Frans' actions."[62]

In the end, Fr. Paolo's burgeoning celebrity status would not be enough to save him. Other priests from the Community had also faced the threat of *Daesh* several times and had different stories to tell. They took different paths, equally brave, but little publicized. "Their priority was for their parishioners," Prof. Loosley states. "Paolo did what he thought was right for the wider Syrian community—but the path taken by the other two [Fr. Frans and Fr. Jacques] was a more meaningful act on a human level for the local communities they were serving."[63]

Fr. Paolo remains a highly charged icon of the Syrian resistance, and a religious figurehead that Assad must regard as equally troublesome in absentia as he was while living in the country. Anyone whose life was touched by Fr. Paolo remembers him with fondness. His larger-than-life personality is indelible in the minds of so many. Sister Houda, an indefatigable stalwart of Mar Musa, describes the profound impact the Italian had on her as a young nun and how he had guided her vocational compass to its true course:

> "During the years of my monastic life—nearly twenty-five—I discovered that it was the will of God that guided me to Deir Mar Musa. My meeting with Paolo—my spiritual master and guide—was what changed the priorities in my life and made them more considered, radical, serious and, in another sense, more Christian. My childish relationship with the beloved Jesus was transformed into a relationship that was more mature, more conscious, and more open to the priorities of our monastery's vocation."[64]

Others reflect nostalgically on the magnetism of the big-hearted Italian. "I am incredibly fond of him and keep hoping he is going to turn up somewhere, someday," says Prof. Loosley

62. Loosley, Interview.

63. Loosley, Interview.

64. Mar Musa, "Newsletter to the friends of Mar Musa," 1–7.

of Fr. Paolo. "He came and stayed with my family some years back. My dad's a retired judge and you don't expect him to be hugging another grown man, both professing their love for each other openly on the streets." Fr. Paolo's small acts of kindness resonated with her family. "My father was later diagnosed with cancer, and Paolo would ring my mother every month to check up on him," she explains. "We all love him dearly. He is like an extended member of the family and yet on a personal level—I began to feel like he thought he was this important actor on the world stage—and, in doing so, he sadly forgot a little bit about the people he had left behind."[65]

Prof. Loosley also recalls the humorous tale of a bet that the Italian made, regarding her own future path. "I recently horrified an old friend of Paolo's by admitting one of the reasons I want to see him again, is to let him know that Sister Houda won a bet made with him almost 20 years ago," she recounts. "Sister Houda told him to stop hassling me about becoming a nun, as it was clear that I would marry and have children. She is now my young child's [Joseph's] godmother. I think we would both like to say 'told you so' to Paolo, if he ever shows up."[66]

Marius Kociejowski has cherished memories of his sojourn in Mar Musa. He remembers the first occasion his wife encountered the dashing Italian, who, at the time, was howling something at some poor bystander, his deep tones ricocheting off the monastery's walls. She exclaimed, "Oh my God! What an Italian!"[67] The sermon he delivered in Mar Musa's little chapel had a profound effect on her. "His [Fr. Paolo's] oration during the mass was remarkable," Kociejowski explains. "They were simple and stripped down sermons that mesmerized with their power. He had a wonderful voice. You clung onto all the words even though you didn't know what they were. My wife is not sympathetic to Catholicism but she

65. Loosley, Interview.
66. Loosley, Interview.
67. Kociejowski, Interview.

described mass in Mar Musa as one of the most moving spiritual experiences of her life."[68]

Many religious figures are active behind the scenes, far from the trumpeting of the media, people who can easily be taken for granted, or even forgotten altogether. People who are *also* heroes, albeit less celebrated, through their own selfless, quiet, toil. "Today the media are not focusing on the good that many religious people are doing," explains Prof. Bongiovanni. "People do risk their lives. Fr. Paolo had a media presence and a special platform for his activities. If he was here, he would also agree that many others are working every day, in small ways—without thanks, without resources—to tackle these challenges."[69]

There are so many figures that we will never know about, men and women, who inspire and lead through their implacable moral courage. People of all creeds and backgrounds, who silently and resolutely make their life's ambition the forging of cross-religious friendships to facilitate dialogue, often in situations of bitter conflict where their safety is far from guaranteed, where recognition is unheard of. One thing remains clear, as close colleague, Gianluca Solera, laments on the emptiness left behind since Fr. Paolo's vanishing, "Yes there is a void. The world needs more people like Paolo. We miss him."[70] Many would wholeheartedly agree.

68. Kociejowski, Interview.
69. Bongiovanni, Interview.
70. Solera, Interview.

Conclusion

The Mar Musa Community won two accolades honoring its work in IFD over the years. The Egypt-based Anna Lindh Euro-Mediterranean Foundation Award for Dialogue between Cultures in 2006; in 2009, the Belgian universities of Louvain and Leuwen awarded Fr. Paolo the title of Doctor Honoris Causa for community action toward Christian-Muslim dialogue.

One hundred years separated Fr. Paolo's and Charles de Foucauld's interfaith activities. During that time, the framework and background to their respective work changed dramatically. The colonial mind-set of curiosity regarding the "otherness" of these exotic lands, and the missionary zeal of civilizing through evangelism has given way to a contemporary fear of the religious *other*. As a result, there is currently a surge in religious stigmatization, polarization, and scapegoating. The antidote seems glaringly obvious—the aim remains true and pressing; there is a need for genuine contact and conversation—not conversion, for dialogue—not distance.

For Fr. Paolo, like de Foucauld and Massignon before him, Islam and Christianity were two sides of the same coin. His islamophilia and affinity with Muslims was a counterweight to the scourge of ever-increasing islamophobia in our world. The unself-conscious and unapologetic love for Islam he celebrated, along with his irreverence for the establishment, won him few adherents in Rome and other Catholic and Christian churches in Syria.

Fr. Paolo's (and Al-Khalil's) theology and interfaith work in Mar Musa, while far from conventional, was a natural progression and fine-tuning of the philosophy of de Foucauld and Massignon, and later of *Lumen Gentium* and the Vatican II decree of *Nostra*

Aetate. It was a decree that had languished in some obscurity for many lonely years, but that Fr. Paolo and his team had vivaciously resurrected and incorporated into their own vocation in Syria.

The tenets of *Nostra Aetate* resonate even more resoundingly today and had no greater promoter than Fr. Paolo. This ethos echoed the rallying call from the church, decades earlier, to put aside interreligious "quarrels and dissensions."[1] It was a chance for Christians to offer up a moral bulwark against the discrimination and scapegoating of "people or any harassment of them on the basis of their race, color, condition in life, or religion."[2] The modern world is in flux. What has played out in Syria over these last few years is simply a microcosm of this.

As we strive to surmount ingrained historical suspicion, ill-will, injustice, and ignorance between various religious tribes, there are many in the West who still view Islam—a religion of over a billion human beings—as backward, dogmatic, radical, *other*. Recently, a steady vilification of Islam and Muslims, amplified by those in the media and positions of authority, has supplanted any sense of logic or compassion. This has dire consequences in its implicit legitimization of extreme positions. It was such crude orientalism that Prof. Edward Said described in an essay published in *The Nation* called "Islam through Western Eyes", long before our polarized post-9/11 reality. He wrote in 1980, "Very little of the detail, the human density, the passion of Arab-Moslem life has entered the awareness of even those people whose profession it is to report the Arab world. What we have, instead, is a series of crude, essentialized caricatures (. . .)"[3]

Little more than a month ago, a gunman walked into two mosques in New Zealand and slaughtered fifty innocent Muslim worshippers. The largest mass killing the country has ever witnessed. As I write this, funerals have already begun for over 250 people butchered in multiple suicide bomb attacks across Sri

1. Second Vatican Council, "Nostra Aetate," paragraph 3.
2. Second Vatican Council, "Nostra Aetate," paragraph 5.
3. Chelala, "Edward Said," lines 24–29.

Lanka. The Islamic State have claimed responsibility for the carnage—apparent revenge for the earlier atrocity.

Increasingly since the 9/11 attack on the World Trade Center in the US, divisive rhetoric has proliferated and filled the vacuum of public discourse. The catastrophic failures of foreign intervention in Afghanistan, Libya, Iraq, and of course Syria, have compounded this. Western involvement in distant lands has been the vile quagmire in which religious extremism has all too easily bred. The ill-conceived economic- and geopolitical-driven neo-colonialism that lies behind the freedom-espousing cheerleading of Western powers to unilaterally invade sovereign states, like Iraq, has, ironically, been the most effective radicalizer and recruiter for the likes of *Daesh* and other Jihadists across the region. The extremists perversely quote the Qur'an to justify their medieval barbarity—mostly against fellow Muslims it must be stressed, not dissimilar to the Lord's Resistance Christian Army in Uganda reciting passages of the bible before heading off to slaughter innocent civilians.

The plan of extremists on both sides is a cynical one. A West that is terrified of Islam and demonizes normal peace-loving Muslims, plays right into the of hands of fringe radicals. It also divides society and sows discontent and mistrust. Consequently, it is easy to see how, within the narrow confines of today's social media echo chambers, Muslims and Islam embody, for some, all that is the very epitome of *other*.

Though relations with Muslims have been affected by the problems of fundamentalism and terrorism, Pope Francis has stressed once again, how important it is to "continue on the dialogue with Islam."[4] Before becoming Pope in 2011, Cardinal Jorge Bergoglio described how pivotal IFD was, in a modern context, in a book called, *On Heaven and Earth*. He stressed that we should not judge others, but instead lay out the carpet of hospitality for all.

4. Bongiovanni, Interview.

"Dialogue is born from an attitude of respect for the other person, from a conviction that the other person has something good to say. It assumes that there is room in the heart for the person's point of view, opinion, and proposal. To dialogue entails a cordial reception, not a prior condemnation. In order to dialogue, it is necessary to know how to lower the defenses, open the doors of the house, and offer human warmth."[5]

Prof. Bongiovanni agrees that *Nostra Aetate*—the "Magna Carta of Dialogue."[6] is still so relevant. A good Christian cannot be selective in what he or she adheres to. It is all or nothing.

"This is not an isolated episode of tolerance from the church. The teachings are still alive and fresh. Many Christians think that IFD might constitute a denial of the mission of the church's proclamation and a sort of negotiation of their faith, a compromise. This is not at all true. When we are engaged in dialogue we do not hide our faith. It is not a watered-down version. There is a lack of education and knowledge as some Christians do not know about *Nostra Aetate*, where the position is very clear. You cannot just take one part and cherry pick. You must take the whole."[7]

The teachings of *Nostra Aetate* are not antithetical to living the life of a good Christian, on the contrary, they very much complement it.

The calamitous war in Syria has instigated a refugee exodus from the region that is unprecedented since the Second World War. Now, more than ever, we must employ Interfaith Dialogue in our own daily lives to combat intolerance closer to home. Good Christians must stop seeing *Nostra Aetate* and IFD as a concession, but rather as the very core of their own faith. Fr. Paolo urged us to abandon our historical suspicion, to fall in love with the *other*.

The values of friendship, love, cooperation and hospitality, so close to the hearts of men like de Foucauld, Massignon, Fr. Jacques,

5. Episcopal Commission, "A Church in Dialogue."

6. Bongiovanni, Interview.

7. Bongiovanni, Interview.

and Fr. Paolo, must be offered unconditionally to those in our nearest orbit who may seem outwardly or inwardly different to us. By a similar measure, we must also offer up these same values, without contempt, to those who seek to demonize others. Rather than ostracizing those who disagree, we must engage with them. The doors to our home *and* minds must be open, like those of Mar Musa; open to dialogue, open to conversation, open to difference. The ideals of *Nostra Aetate* should surround us in our own lives, guiding our thoughts, our actions, our behavior; a shield against hate.

There is no better time for us to be vocal and fearless exponents of the miracle of dialogue—like the kind espoused by Fr. Paolo, the Community of Al-Khalil, and Mar Musa. Undoubtedly, this remains challenging for it is dialogue against the odds. In our own lives, through our schools, universities and cultural institutions, we can positively channel the pivotal message at the heart of Mar Musa's unique IFD. True and fearless proponents of IFD are people who embody both the words and the spirit of *Nostra Aetate*. Christian society must reacquaint itself with the ideas contained therein and start living them by re-disseminating and popularizing its message among the faithful. The flourishing hubs of rich intercultural and religious learning which Fr. Paolo and his religious team nurtured, spiritual crossroads of humanity like Mar Musa, should not be an anomaly on the religious landscape of any country. Based on the ideals set forth in *Nostra Aetate*, they should be the norm.

Anyone in doubt about the practical application of the principles of *Nostra Aetate* need only ask Fr. Jacques from Mar Elian, who was kidnapped by *Daesh*. Could non-violence and dialogue be a realistic and viable path forward against the barbarity of the likes of *Daesh*? He was candid about whether dialogue offered any practical solution to the scourge of sectarian wars that continue to terrorize the region. "The solution cannot simply be eliminating those who persecute us. The only way of stopping the extremists is to enter into a dialogue with Islam. That has been my personal experience," states Fr. Jacques, who has looked calmly into the eyes of his *Daesh* captors during his 5-month-long ordeal of torture and mistreatment in 2015. "We—all the Christians of my old parish—decided *not* to resort to violence, despite the danger. That is why we are still alive. A *Daesh* commander told me exactly that. Last spring, I had the following inspiration during Mass: our world needs a *revolution against violence*. Only then will it be able to find peace. We want to be instruments of peace."[8] It eloquently exemplified everything that Fr. Paolo and Al-Khalil stand for.

8. Pelster, "Syrian Priest Who Escaped ISIS," line 30–44.

Epilogue

AT THE FINAL STAGES of researching this book, in February 2019, I found myself in Iraqi Kurdistan visiting the Community of Deir Maryam al-Adhra in Sulaymaniyah. I spent several wonderful weeks there with Fr. Jens and his team. Mere days after arriving, I was stunned to learn of a report in the British press, from an unnamed Kurdish source, that alleged Fr. Paolo was alive and being held as a hostage by *Daesh* in the last Syrian enclave of their ravaged caliphate—Baghuz. A torrent of thoughts immediately besieged my mind, if it indeed turned out to be true, yet how joyous to have him come back from the dead like that. He would appreciate the irony that at the end of a research project speculating on his "legacy," he would suddenly reappear, Lazarus-like, finger wagging, spanner in hand, with plenty of suggested redactions.

I, like many others, had been led to believe, with almost grim certainty, that there was little chance of him ever turning up alive. What a twist to his tale that would be. Sadly, only the next day, the very same reports were refuted by other Kurdish sources. And so the fickle tide of hope and despair cruelly ebbed and flow, such is the pendulum of fate and the intensity of emotions that well up inside the loved ones and friends of the missing at times like this.

As the war reaches its endgame stage in Syria, there will undoubtedly be a pressing need for restorative and reconciliatory post-conflict IFD work that sets about redressing the pain and loss, as well as healing some of the deep sectarian wounds that the war has inflicted on communities. This must be true dialogue that focuses on peacebuilding between the disparate religious tribes, harnessing individuals' participation and their personal experience through storytelling. In this way survivors can delve deeper and seek out the highs and lows of their shared experiences of conflict. That may involve tackling sensitive political issues and points of social justice, where participants confess, share tragic events, and even seek forgiveness.

Not everyone is responsible for acts committed in the name of their religion, but for dialogue with the clear goal of reconciliation, these steps are crucial. Cardinal Arinze, Cardinal Bishop of Velletri-Segni since 2005, writes that "Acceptance of fault where it exists, willingness to engage in self-criticism, asking and giving pardon, and willingness to seek reconciliation are virtues badly needed for true and lasting peace."[1] This does not magically make problems disappear, but it at least acknowledges responsibility— the first step on the path of healing. Christianity extolls atonement to sinners. In Islam, the Qur'an repeatedly references Allah's mercy—stressing the cathartic power of forgiveness.

It is imperative that dialogue is promptly undertaken in any society reeling after a sustained period of war. It would be hugely worthwhile to investigate the effectiveness of IFD in a purely Syrian context. A traumatized and scarred post-conflict society could benefit from the healing embrace of IFD's efforts.

1. Cox and Philpot in Abu-Nimer et al., *Unity in Diversity*, 22.

Current Situation Across the Community of Al-Khalil

Monastery of Deir Mar Elian Al-Qaryatayn, Syria

This monastery is run by Fr. Jacques Mourad. He was responsible for initiating various cross-religious community reconstruction projects after battles destroyed local homes and infrastructure. Located in the town of al-Qaryatayn, about 100km southeast of Homs, Deir Mar Elian also became a refuge during some of the fiercest fighting of the Syrian Civil War. Up to 50 families—Muslim and Christian—sought shelter in the safe surrounds of the monastery's walls for up to three months. In May of 2015, Fr. Jacques was abducted by *Daesh* militants and held captive for almost five months. He luckily managed to escape after a sustained period of mistreatment. In August of that same year, *Daesh* captured the town and completely destroyed the monastery and the shrine of Mar Elian. The shrine was a chapel housing the Byzantine sarcophagus of Mar Elian. *Daesh* smashed the sarcophagus and scattered the bones inside.

The city was later liberated by Syrian government forces in April 2016. Sadly, the monastery still remains in complete ruin and successive fighting in the area has compounded the devastation. It is now in a state of abandon, its church crumbling, the rooms charred and blackened. The parish church in the town has been burnt and damaged in many parts. Although people are beginning to return to Al-Qaryatayn, numbers are limited. Recently, 200 families returned and some have said that this number will increase to 700 families with the re-opening of the school.

Amongst these, only one Christian family has come back. Christians are concerned for they do not know what their future will be in the region. The majority of Christians in the region live in the two villages of Fairuzeh and Zaidal, near Homs. The Al-Khalil community is actively involved in getting help to these internal refugees who are in need. Great effort is also being made to carry on with the agricultural projects of Mar Elian to save what is savable: irrigating the olives which are still more or less alive, and the vines—most of which have died. Unfortunately, all the fruit trees in the surrounds of the monastery have withered. They have not found anyone to help them with this work because of the ongoing threat of *Daesh*. Fr. Jacques is not in Al-Qaryatayn anymore. No one is there now. After liberation, *Daesh* returned several times to the town and killed over 200 Muslims.[2] 2019 brings new hope that life can start to return to normal in the town without the omnipresent threat of extremism.

Deir Maryam al-Adhra, Monastery of the Virgin Mary, Sulaymaniyah, Iraq

In operation since 2011, under the leadership of Fr. Jens, Fr. Jacques, and Sister Friederike, Deir Maryam continues its generous and patient care of the refugees in the surrounding area of the monastery who have been displaced and seek shelter. As of 2017—the monastery has returned to a relative state of calm after the transfer of several displaced families from parts of Syria and Mosul into prefabricated housing. The monastery created two caravan villages next to the church in order to guarantee greater autonomy and privacy to each family.

The monastery fills every day with children and adults coming from various parts of the city in order to take part in courses which are organized in its precincts. English courses and various activities for the children, obligatory courses of Kurdish for young and old, sewing courses for Christian and Muslim women, the

2. Anonymous, Interview.

summer camp *Children of Light* under the guidance of Fr. Jacques, theatre workshops, and a theatre group led by Sister Friederike. They also organize more practical workshops based around various trades. After consulting with some local companies, they saw the need to teach the skills of interior decorating, electrical and plumbing installation, welding, sewing, and secretarial/office skills. Amongst those teaching are refugees, including volunteer Kurdish and foreign teachers. They have just begun to finish, with European financing, a new wing next to the church which is intended for accommodating nuns and female guests. They are beginning to compile a library but books are needed.

Monastery of San Salvatore, Cori, Italy

The monastery in Cori was set up for the academic formation of the Community. It was used as a center of study and learning until the war. It has an academic focus, but is also a place of refuge for members of the Community that cannot stay in Syria because they are European and threatened by *Daesh*.

Monastery of Mar Musa al-Habashi, Nebek, Syria

During the spring of 2017, the valley at the foot of the monastery was dressed in an enchanting red gown of bright crimson poppies, scattered to the horizon. With the cessation of hostilities in the surrounding area, the Community at last experienced, for the first time after many long years of war, enormous joy at seeing the entrance of the road to the monastery full of activity and movement; many families from Nebek are again coming to visit them. Fridays are the day when they again receive hundreds of guests. What a joy it was for the monks and nuns who stayed on in Mar Musa to see Christian and Muslim families once again climbing up the stone steps together to receive the blessing of this sacred place. Young Muslim men and women from Nebek come to proudly show off *their* monastery to Christian friends and colleagues from other areas. Muslim women again approach the monastery's Sisters to ask for prayers for their intention.

Recently parts of the monastery have been restored to not only make the Community more prepared for offering hospitality to visiting pilgrims, but to also offer an atmosphere of silence and meditation to those who seek it.

The monks and nuns continue their normal daily tasks with guests' help. Some of them take daily care of the little garden, which gives a bounty of medicinal and aromatic plants, while the olive trees have provided an abundant harvest once again. The production of good cheese under the management of Brother Boutros helps to foster good relations with the shepherds of the area from whom they buy milk. Brother Yause continues the production of candles and will soon begin to develop a project to craft artisan candles. Sister Houda continues the supervision and direction of projects of the Community, while Sister Deema assists in various correspondence tasks.

The Community continues, with the support of friends and foundations, to help the refugee families of the city of Al-Qary-atayn. In collaboration with a team of lay people, and under the direction of the local parish priest of Fairuze, the community tries to understand what their essential needs are. Special thought is given to those who are unable to provide basic necessities to their own families (rent, milk for babies, etc.).

Students are a priority and the Community help parents provide school materials for children and university students. Health issues and the cost of medical supplies are some of the most pressing challenges that need to be addressed. With the aid of fundraising and donors in Italy, the Community has helped extend services at the hospital of Nebek, including vital medicine and equipment. A music school project has also been initiated between Muslim and Christians in Nebek. The community oversees a nursery school, which, in addition to its educational focus, organizes sessions of psychological assistance with experts who give advice on how to confront the severe psychological problems caused by war and PTSD.

If you would like to make a financial contribution to the Community to help them in their ongoing work (please mark donations "for Mar Musa"), you can do so through the following website: https://magis.gesuiti.it/10585-2/.

Bibliography

Abu-Nimer, Khoury, et al. *Unity in Diversity: Interfaith Dialogue in the Middle East*. Washington: United States Institute of Peace, 2007.

Alam, M.K. Interview, 2018.

Annan, Koffi. "Syrian Peace Plan." https://en.wikipedia.org/wiki/Kofi_Annan_Syrian_peace_plan

Anonymous, Interview, 2018.

Bashir, Interview, 2018–2019.

Bongiovanni, Ambrogio. Interview, 2018.

Buck, Dorothy. *Louis Massignon: A Pioneer of Interfaith Dialogue*. New Jersey: Blue Dome, 2017.

Chaillot, Christine. *The Syrian Orthodox Church of Antioch and all the East: A Brief Introduction to its Life and Spirituality*. Geneva: Inter-Orthodox Dialogue, 1998.

Chelala, Cesar. "Edward Said: Remembering a Palestinian Patriot." https://www.commondreams.org/views/2019/04/10/edward-said-remembering-palestinian-patriot

Cockburn, Patrick. "Desperate Assad Tries to Blunt Uprising with New Promises of Reform." https://www.independent.co.uk/news/world/middle-east/desperate-assad-tries-to-blunt-uprising-with-new-promises-of-reform-2254771.html

COSV Comitato di Coordinoento Delle Organizzazioni per il Servisio Voluntario "Deir Mar Musa Documentary," 2011. https://www.youtube.com/watch?v=7tfq-3u3hG8

Dall'Oglio, Paolo. "In Praise of Syncretism." Translation Thomas Michel SJ, http://www.westcoastcompanions.org/jgc/1.2/dallogliotext.htm

Dall'Oglio, Paolo. *Innamorato dell'Islam, credente in Gesù. Dell'islamofilia*. Italy: Jaca Book, 2011.

Dall'Oglio, Paolo. "*Syrian Diaries*." http://www.popoli.info/EasyNe2/Idee/Di_nuovo_in_Siria.aspx

Dall'Oglio, Paolo. "Interview on Al Arabiya." News Channel Studio Beirut, by Giselle Khoury, June, 2012. https://youtu.be/1rO3wqe-twM

De Nicolas, Antonio. *Ignatius De Loyola, Powers of Imagining: A Philosophical Hermeneutic of Imagining Through the Collected Works of Ignatius De Loyola*. New York: State University New York, 1986.

Doyle, Dennis M. "The Concept of Inculturation in Roman Catholicism: A Theo-logical Consideration," Religious Studies Faculty Publications. Paper, 2012.

Episcopal Commission for Christian Unity, "A Church in Dialogue: The Catholic Church and Interreligious Dialogue," 2015. http://www.cccb.ca/ site/images/stories/pdf/Nostra_Aetate_-_50th_Anniversary.pdf

Erlich, Reese. *Inside Syria: The Backstory of their Civil War and What the World Can Expect.* New York: Prometheus, 2014.

Falciatori, Samantha. "Who-is-father-Dall'Oglio-the-jesuit-abducted-in-syria-2-years-ago?" https://wewritewhatwelike.com/2015/07/31/

Fedda, Yasmin. *A Tale of Two Syrias.* Tell Brak Films Production, Translation Azzam & Fedda, London: 2012.

Fisk, Robert. "Every Concession Makes the President More Vulnerable." https:// www.independent.co.uk/voices/commentators/fisk/robert-fisk-every-concession-makes-the-president-more-vulnerable-2273755.html

Fisk, Robert. "Out of Syria's Darkness Come Tales of Terror." https://www. independent.co.uk/voices/commentators/fisk/robert-fisk-out-of-syrias-darkness-come-tales-of-terror-2276392.html

Fisk, Robert. "Syria Slips Towards Sectarian War." https://www.independent. co.uk/voices/commentators/fisk/robert-fisk-syria-slips-towards-sectarian-war-2376408.html

Gagliarduci, Andrea. "In Syrian Monastery Priest Who Escaped ISIS Sees Signs of Hope." https://www.catholicnewsagency.com/news/in-syrian-monastery-priest-who-escaped-isis-sees-signs-of-hope-69282

Hamadi, Shady. Interview, 2018.

Kociejowski, Marius. Interview, 2019.

Kociejowski, Marius. *Zaroaster's Children.* Windsor, Ontario: Biblioasis, 2015.

Kwiatkowski SJ, Zygmunt. *Życie Między Pustyniami: Mar Musa al Habashi.* Krakow: Wydawnictwo Krakow, 2015.

Landis, Joshua. "Islamic Education in Syria: Undoing Secularism." http:// tinyurl.com/2kj84j.

Leverett, Flynt. *Inheriting Syria: Bashar's Trial by Fire.* Washington: Brookings Institute, 2005.

Loosley, Emma. "The Community of Al-Khalil: Monastic Life in the Service of Christian-Islamic Dialogue." Paper, 2004. https://www.academia. edu/11425502/The_Community_of_Al-Khalil_Monastic_Life_in_the_ Service_of_Christian-Islamic_Dialogue

Loosley, Emma. Interview, 2019.

Mar Musa Community, "Newsletter to the Friends of Mar Musa." 2017.

Mass, Warren. "Jesuit Priest Murdered in Syrian City of Homs." https:// www.thenewamerican.com/world-news/asia/item/18009-jesuit-priest-murdered-in-syrian-city-of-homs

Merad, Ali. *Christian Hermit in an Islamic World: A Muslim's View of Charles de Foucauld.* Translated by Zoe Hersov. New Jersey: Paulist, 1999.

Moss, Robert Tewdwr. *Cleopatra's Wedding Present: Travels through Syria.* London: Duckworth, 1998.

O'Malley SJ, John W., "Vatican II Revisited as Reconciliation: The Francis Factor" in *The Legacy of Vatican II.* edited by Fagioli and Vacini, 1–23. New Jersey: Paulist, 2015.

Pelster, Berthold. "Syrian Priest Who Escaped ISIS: 'Our World Needs a Revolution Against Violence.'" https://www.catholicnewsagency.com/news/syrian-priest-who-escaped-isis-our-world-needs-a-revolution-against-violence-98159

Petzold, Fr. Jens. Interview, 2019

Second Vatican Council, "Nostra Aetate: Declaration on the Relation of the Church to NonChristian Religions." Rome: 1965.

Solera, Gianluca. Interview, 2018.

Szanto Ali-Dib, Edith. "Inter-Religious Dialogue in Syria: Politics, Ethics and Miscommunication." MA Thesis, University of Toronto, 2008. https://www.academia.edu/465177/Inter-Religious_Dialogue_in_Syria_Politics_Ethics_and_Miscommunication

Szanto, Edith. Interview, 2019.

Van Dam, Nikolaos. *The Struggle for Power in Syria: Politics and Society Under Asad and the Ba'th Party.* New York: I.B. Tauris, 2011.

Yassin-Kassab, Robin., and Leila Al-Shami. *Burning Country: Syrians in Revolution and War.* London: Pluto, 2016.

Yildiz, Kerim. *The Kurds in Iraq: The Past, Present and Future.* London: Pluto, 2004.

Youssef, Interview, 2019.